THE RECRUITMENT STARTUP SUCCESS PLAN

JOSH WELLMAN

First Printed in Great Britain by
Obex Publishing Ltd in 2020

1 2 4 6 8 10 9 7 5 3

Paperback ISBN: 978-1-913454-32-6
Hardback ISBN: 978-1-913454-38-8
eBook ISBN: 978-1-913454-33-3

A CIP catalogue record for this book is available
from the British Library

Obex Publishing Limited
Reg. No. **12169917**

Table of Contents

Introduction 5

PART 1 STARTING YOUR RECRUITMENT COMPANY ... 8

Chapter 1: What is a Recruitment Company? 9

Chapter 2: Business Basics...20

Chapter 3: Legal Milestones to Cover 40

Chapter 4: Creating an Online Presence 47

Chapter 5: The Importance of GDPR And Your
Responsibilities..62

PART 2 - RUNNING A SUCCESSFUL RECRUITMENT
COMPANY...80

Chapter 1: What Are Your Aims? 81

Chapter 2: Set Your Fees Competitively................................87

Chapter 3: Building Strong Working Relationships 97

Chapter 4: 10 Office Tips to Boost Your Productivity........105

Chapter 5: 10 Recruitment-Specific Good Practice Tips to
Use at All Times 113

PART 3 - GROWING YOUR BUSINESS 121

Chapter 1: The Importance of Staying Relevant.................122

Chapter 2: 8 Tips to Expand Your Recruitment Agency 130

Chapter 3: How Key Performance Indicators (KPIs) Can Help
You...141

Chapter 4: Four Simple Steps to Business Growth.............147

Conclusion 155

Introduction

Establishing and starting any kind of business requires careful planning and a lot of research. If you want to ensure that you tick all the necessary boxes and cover any red tape you need to be covered, it's vital that you do your homework before making a move.

It's extremely easy to miss a detail that seems small, but a few months down the line it turns into something that could derail your efforts and lead your business towards failure. In that case, research is key and listening to advice also.

Competition is fierce in the recruitment industry and the smallest thing could trip up your efforts. Legal requirements, paperwork, making life easier, and ensuring you have all the necessary systems in place, these are vital parts of the puzzle. It's hard to find reliable information, but sticking with the official word is important.

That's where this book comes in.

This book covers everything you need to know about setting up a recruitment agency from the start, and what to do to give you the best shot at overall success. Then, we'll talk about how to maintain that success, moving towards future growth.

It might seem like a mountain to climb right now, but laying the foundations in the strongest possible manner is vital if you want to ensure you don't run into problems further down the line. You also need to know the recruitment industry inside and out. This is an industry that is far-reaching, complicated, fiercely competitive, and extremely rewarding. It is also very fast-moving and things don't stay still for very long. If you want to stay afloat, you need to be up to date with all the latest news and developments, and if you want your business to grow, you need to act upon those developments quickly and carefully.

The best advice is to read this book from start to finish, even if you haven't even chosen a name for your new business yet. Then, note down everything you need to do and create a flow chart of sorts. By doing that, you won't miss anything and you'll be able to plan out the coming months in a way which will give you the best possible shot at future success. There is probably far more to do than you realise right now, but creating a clear route on paper will show you the way through and simplify things, so you don't miss anything vital.

This book is divided into three parts. The first part covers how to set up your business, the second part talks about how to not only have a recruitment business of your own but how to run a successful one. The third part covers how to take your company a step further and grow it into something which is going to stand the test of time. Each step is equally as challenging as the next but in extremely different ways. You need to be diverse, flexible, hard working, resilient, and aware to succeed in the recruitment industry, no matter what stage of the game you're currently at.

First of all, let's cover the basics. If you want to learn something from scratch, you need to know the foundations, i.e. what a recruitment business is, what it does, what it doesn't do, and why it's a vital cog in the wheel of today's business world.

Let's begin.

PART 1

STARTING YOUR
RECRUITMENT COMPANY

Chapter 1:

What is a Recruitment Company?

You might sometimes hear a recruitment company referred to as an employment agency, but they are one and the same thing. The main focus is sourcing out high quality talent for companies to employ. Of course, this means developing strong working relationships with both clients and candidates, treating people well, and ensuring that you stay up to date with whatever is going on in the industry at the same time.

Because much of the work a recruitment company does is on both sides, it's important to have systems in place to ensure that nothing gets missed. You cannot focus too much on clients, e.g. businesses who need people to fill their job vacancies, and then neglect the candidates, e.g. the people you're representing and trying to help them fulfil their career dreams.

Let's simplify this down:

- A recruitment company helps to match potential candidates to vacancies within a company
- A recruitment company works with companies to find the best candidates for their vacancies too

Effective focus on both sides means happy clients and candidates, and clients are more likely to use your services in the future when they need to look towards filling a new vacancy. They are also more likely to refer you to their colleagues and perhaps other companies who need recruitment services. There are countless new and established recruitment companies in the industry at any one time, so staying one step ahead is vital for success and growth.

Recruitment companies also look for potential vacancies and opportunities, helping businesses to identify where a new role may be necessary, and streamlining the recruitment process overall.

If you've ever tried to fill a vacancy before, you'll understand how long-winded, tedious and costly the whole process can be. In the end, you cannot be 100% sure that you've chosen a person who is going to fulfil their potential within the role, or someone who is actually as high quality as they claim to be. When working with a recruitment company, businesses have this worry taken away, because candidates are screened by the agency and matched to the types of roles which suit their skills and experience best. The guess work is taken out of the equation, and there is more of a certainty that this is going to be the best person for the job.

All of this equals less time spent on recruitment, less cost, less need to go back over the whole process because it wasn't done correctly in the first place, and a smoother transition when the successful candidate starts their new role. This means no loss of time or productivity for the business, and gives them a better chance at growth for their own company that particular year.

From a candidate's point of view, a recruitment company helps to find the best type of opportunities for them, according to their past experience, their skills, and what they're looking for in their career. They also offer help with CV writing and give advice on how to excel during an interview. These services help to push candidates forward and prepare them for employment in the best type of role for them. It is the recruiter's job to identify what type of job they would excel in and sell the vacancy to the candidate and encourage them to apply.

As a recruitment company becomes more successful, businesses will go to them for their services, however, at first, you will need to be prepared to hustle a little. This means calling around companies, doing your homework, selling your services and ensuring that you keep your new client as happy as possible, finding them the candidate they need, in a timely manner.

Once a client signs up with the recruitment company, the search begins for the ideal candidate. This means the company will look at their database and see if they have anyone who matches the company's requirements. If so, they will be contacted and given information about the vacancy, encouraging them to apply.

The company will also put out an advertisement in the most pertinent places, to help attract the right candidates, and may even head-hunt high-class talent they're aware of and who may be perfect for the role. Once they have received several applications, the shortlisting process will begin.

The company itself may do the short-listing and interviewing, but it could be that businesses themselves want a hand in things. It's up to the recruitment company to find the best way forward for their client and help ensure that they're happy at every stage of the recruitment process.

For some contracts, once a suitable client has been selected from the interview, the process may end there. The business may want to do the drawing up of a contract and offer letters themselves. However, not all businesses have the time to do this, and in that case, this is an extra service that a quality recruitment company can offer to their clients.

Obviously, the greater scope of services you can offer, the more you are going to attract new and impressive companies your way.

We should also point out that candidates are able to sign up with several recruitment companies at any one time, giving them a greater chance at finding suitable and successful employment. That means that you're constantly working against the clock, always competing against other agencies, some of which you may not even be aware of; a candidate isn't at liberty to tell you whether they're working with another agency or not.

Having fast-acting yet comprehensive processes in place is therefore vital if you want to ensure that you catch the best talent out there, and help them to be hired in a vacancy that you're working with. Then, you receive your fee, the client is happy, and the candidate is over the moon. It sounds simple, but it involves a series of actions that need to be timed to perfection and carried out extremely carefully. That's the thrill of recruitment!

The Scope For Success Explained

So, why are recruitment companies so in demand right now?

We've touched upon this, but businesses do not have the time or money to risk on candidates that may not be ideal. Not all businesses have a dedicated recruitment department, and if they do, this could be a hugely expensive endeavour to run. In that case, using the services of a recruitment agency could be a better option, saving money and time in the process of finding the best talent for a role. It's also far better to work with a company who have these specialist skills, creating a smoother process and giving the client a far better chance at identifying a person for the role who is going to fit into the existing business with ease, learn quickly, and hit the ground running.

Recruitment companies are more likely to be able to unearth hidden gems, e.g. talent which is 100% perfect for a role. They can do this because it's their job to - they can recruit potential candidates who have been making waves in their particular industry and they do this by keeping their ear to the ground and knowing who should and shouldn't be on their radar. Then, they contact that person and persuade them to sign up and look for roles that are more in-keeping with their career goals and aspirations.

Recruitment is extremely lengthy and unless you know the ins and outs of the entire industry, it's easy to make mistakes. That's one of the main reasons why businesses choose to work with recruitment companies rather than try and do it all themselves. This frees them up to concentrate on running their business and doing what they know best. That means no loss of productivity, no loss of profit, and no damaging effects on growth.

Put simply, recruitment companies help to cut down on the chances of wasting time and money on a lost cause. It's easy to impress on a CV and at interview, but that doesn't always mean that the person chosen is going to quickly slide into the position and excel from the get-go. Of course, a recruitment company can't guarantee this either, but the chances are far higher because they work with the candidate and get to know them far better than a company has the time to do.

The money that a business will pay a recruitment company to take the hard work out of the equation is therefore far lower than a mistake made and ten times easier too. For that reason, recruitment companies are in high demand, hence why there are so many of them in the industry at the current time, with more and more establishing themselves every year.

The Importance of Covering All Bases

There is one thing you should be very aware of - recruitment is a cutthroat, highly competitive business and the sheer number of recruitment companies establishing themselves yearly means that you're going to have to work very hard for the contracts and candidates you find.

You can use this to push yourself to further success or you can allow it to drown you. It's always better to choose the first option! Being aware of what you're getting yourself into means that you're not going to be shocked at how hard you have to work to find the ideal matches for vacancies. It's a thrill, something to work hard towards, and when you find the ideal fit, it's rewarding too.

Because of that competition, that means you need to cover every single base, from the moment you decide to set up a recruitment company to the time when you're established and receiving a steady amount of work. Failing to make careful, measured decisions means that you're risking losing a client because of a small problem. The amount of competition means that just one small mistake or misunderstanding could derail everything.

Never underestimate the power of word of mouth. Companies can easily be put off working with you due to one or two bad reviews, or because someone they know has worked with you in the past and they didn't rate the service you provided. It could be something as small as not being as polite as perhaps you could have been, and it's enough to cause you to lose out on several contracts as a result.

Recruitment companies have to be on point if they want to be successful and that means covering every single base. Luckily, by working carefully when you start your business, you'll have processes and mechanisms in place to ensure that doesn't happen.

In the second part of this book, we're going to talk about some useful tips that will help make your days easier and therefore free up some time to focus on quality, rather than just ticking along. However, the first part, actually setting up your business, is something you need to be extremely careful about too. Not following the rules on one very small detail could come back to bite you at a later time and trying to rectify it later on will be ten times harder than at the start. This is the same when setting up any type of business but the sheer competition in the recruitment industry means that you need to ensure that there are no loose ends left untied.

It might be time consuming at the start, but it's worth it.

Do Your Homework

The final point to mention is that working in recruitment requires a lot of research.

At the start, you'll need to research everything you need to do in order to complete the establishment of your company, but as you become more successful you'll see that you need to research companies, and create a unique selling point (USP) which helps you stand out amongst the rest. This means highlighting gaps in their service where a new recruit could be useful and selling that idea to the company.

It means headhunting the best talent there is, and knowing who to target.

Recruitment isn't just the ticking along of a daily routine, it's stretching yourself and looking for opportunities. It's about identifying needs when the people concerned might not have the first idea that they need something in the first place. You have to be the one to convince them that they do, and put forward a very convincing argument to back up your claims.

All of this means that creating a recruitment company from scratch is hard work. Is it rewarding? Certainly. At the end of the day, you're helping people advance their careers, perhaps even helping their dreams come true. You're also playing a part in the growth of a company, by helping identify the right people for their vacancies.

It's quite likely that you already know a fair amount about recruitment, given the fact that you're thinking about starting your own recruitment company. However, it's vital to go over the basics at the start of any endeavour. Covering the foundation means that you can build upon it in the strongest and most stable of ways. Perhaps you might have had a slightly wrong idea in your mind about what a recruitment company really does, or maybe you didn't realise how much homework would be involved in the day to day running of the company, in order to ensure it's a success. Now you know.

So, with the basics covered, let's move on to the business basics you need to know. Our next chapter is a lengthy one, but it's going to give you all the information you need to set up your business from a legal and red tape point of view. Make sure you cover every single point in this next chapter, to ensure that you're not going to fall foul of a basic, yet costly, mistake later on.

Chapter 2:

Business Basics

You have a vision of what you want your company to be like, but in order to get started, you need to actually create the company from a legal point of view.

A company needs to be named, registered, and all tax and VAT points covered before you are legally able to start trading. Failure to cover any of the most important business basics could result in time lost, but could also result in a very hefty fine, or possibly even worse. The good news is that these basics are pretty easy to do and don't take up a huge amount of time.

However, it's a good idea to take your time when moving through the various stages and choosing the options you go with carefully. For instance, choosing the wrong accountant could mean that you waste time and money further down the line. Not opening the best type of business account for your recruitment company could mean that you struggle to receive certain types of payments, or that you find it difficult to transfer money overseas, if you ever need to.

We mentioned the word 'homework' in our last chapter and you'll need to do an awful lot of that before making many of the basic business decisions in front of you. However, take heart in the fact that working slowly at this point will set you up for success in the future.

Create Your Business Plan

The first step towards setting up your business is to create an in-depth business plan.

A business plan outlines everything about your business, what your projected earnings are, and what you are planning on achieving in a set number of years later. If you need to seek out extra funding for your business, the bank or other loaning company will definitely ask to see your business plan. This document forms the backbone of your new business, so it needs to be as comprehensive as possible.

You can find templates online to base your business plan on, but it's best to be as unique as you can and make the plan completely personalised to your business endeavours. The main areas you need to cover are:

- **Information about you as the owner** - Talk about why you want to run a recruitment company and what makes you the ideal person to have this type of business.

- **Information about your business** - Be clear what type of recruitment company you want to run. Are you going to spread out into international recruitment? Are you going to stick to full time opportunities or are you going to look into part time recruitment opportunities too? Are you going to specialise in different niches or are you going to be general and work across a range of areas? You will also need to explain how many employees you want to take on, how much you plan on paying them, and where they will work.
- **Business base information** - You need a business address, i.e. where your business is going to run from. This doesn't have to be a huge office space, but you need a specific and eligible address that will be the registered base for your business.
- **Financial details** - How will you fund your recruitment business? Do you have savings? Are you going to ask for funding from the bank? Do you have a business partner who is going to inject capital into the business? Make sure you include as much detail here as possible, especially if you're looking to borrow capital to get your business off the ground.
- **Market research information to back up your business plan** - Before you even start putting your business plan together, you will have done some research into the demand for your new recruitment company. You need to include this in

your business plan, as it shows that there is a viable need for a business such as this. Again, if you're looking to borrow capital, this part is very important. Include information on the other recruitment companies in your local area and those who you believe will be your direct competitors. Talk about your specific target audience and why they need your business to be in existence. You also need to identify a unique selling points (USP), which shows how your business is going to stand out amongst your competitors.

- **Projected profits and costs of running the business** - Whilst you can't be 100% accurate at this point, you will need to include information, based on your market research, which projects your outgoings for the first year, the first two years, and possibly up to the fifth year. You also need to project your profits, and hopefully, show them on an upwards trajectory. Be sure to include all potential outgoings, and don't be tempted to shave a few off to make your business plan look better - this needs to be realistic and 100% accurate to ensure that your business has the best chance of success.

Once you have your business plan in place, you have a clear idea of what you want your recruitment company to look like and how you think it is going to run. Of course, things might change and you might tweak a few ideas after you've been trading for a short while, but for now, this plan is your 'get it off the ground' go-to route and if you need to ask for funding, it will be the number one document potential lenders want to see.

As a result, don't rush your business plan and make sure that you include as much detail as possible. You should remember to include all potential losses and costs, as this not only helps it to look more realistic, but it helps you to plan to overcome these inevitable first or second year bumps which are certainly going to come the way of any new business, in any niche.

Identifying Your Company Name

Before you can move on with any other part of the process of setting up your recruitment company officially, you need something to call it. This might sound like the easy part, but it's surprisingly difficult!

Remember, this is the name you're going to be stuck with for the remainder of the days your business is ticking along, which will hopefully be many more years. The name also needs to be professional yet something which stands out, it also needs to be make it clear anyone who hears the name what you're about, i.e. that you're a recruitment company.

You will need to do some research to check that your prospective name is actually legal - there are some names that cannot be used, so make sure you do your homework ahead of time. You should then check the name isn't used by someone else already and that it's available for you.

Come up with a shortlist of names and then head to the Companies House website and run a check on the names you have noted down. You'll find yourself in hot water if you move ahead with a name that is already taken, so it's best to cut out the hard work and ensure that your name is available at the start.

When choosing your name from the shortlist you've created, remember that people will look at the name and form a first impression from the get-go. It's very difficult to change someone's first impression of you and it's best to do all you can to impress from the start. Make sure that you're conveying a message of professionalism but also personality. The name should also show that you're quite easy to work with; businesses don't want to work with a recruitment company that makes life harder than it needs to be, so if you can show your easy going nature in your name, that would stand you in good stead.

You should also keep an eye on the future. What are your plans for your business over the long-term? This might be impacted by the name you choose to keep this in mind. For instance, if you want to grow your business over the years, you shouldn't be too rigid. If you choose something which implies you are a specialist recruitment company and in the future, you want to branch out into other niches or perhaps be more generalised, you're going to struggle and perhaps need to change your name once more. That is time and money lost.

A final point concerns growth into international markets. If you are going to work with overseas clients, you need to ensure that the name you're choosing doesn't translate into anything either confusing or even offensive.

A name is never just a name and it's worthwhile taking your time finding the right fit, to save time, hassle and money in the long-run.

How to Create a Limited Company

The single best option to get you started on your road to recruitment success is to set up a limited company from the get-go.

A limited company is a private company and gives you protection against any money-related issues in the future. A limited company means that the owners, i.e. you, are only responsible for any money or debts owed by the business, to the amount they actually invested in the first place.

Of course, nobody wants to think about their shiny new business possibly going bankrupt, but it's prudent to protect yourself any untoward incidents in the future. By creating a limited company, you're ensuring that you're only going to be liable to whatever you started with, and nothing past that point is your responsibility - not your home, your cars, or anything else you own.

Whilst every business has to take risks in order to survive and grow, there is always the potential downside of failure. Creating a limited company, therefore, gives you peace of mind and allows you to take measured business risks without sleepless nights worrying about the consequences should things go wrong.

There are a few other benefits of setting up a limited company too:

- Protects you against untoward financial consequences
- Helps with tax and other financial owing, due to efficiency

- Helps to give your business credibility and increases your reputation as a result - the recruitment agency hinges on a good reputation

Setting up a limited company is quite easy. You'll need the following information to hand:

- An official address for your business - Make sure that the address is actually eligible to be a business address first and foremost; some residential addresses cannot be used for business purposes
- A name for your business - As before, check this is available and legal
- Register with Companies House - To do this you will need your details, capital details, the currency you are going to trade in and any stocks or shares held and you will need to pay a small registration fee at the time. The process takes no more than 15 minutes.

It's that easy.

It's possible to register your business for corporation tax whilst registering with Companies House, which could save you time. However, you don't have to take this step right now. If you don't, remember to register with HMRC (HM Revenue and Customs) for your tax concerns afterward. Do not delay this step and certainly do not forget it!

Once you have a name and your business is registered, you are halfway there. You now have an official, registered recruitment company of your own and the next steps ensure that you're making your own life easier for the coming weeks and years. Again, take your time with this process and ensure that you tick all necessary boxes. In terms of tax issues, not registering in time or missing out important details could mean that you end up owing money at the end of the tax year and you're also risking a considerable fine too.

How to Find a Quality Accountant, And What They Can do For You

A high quality accountant will make the running of your business far more streamlined and accurate. You will also have peace of mind that you're not missing any important details, such as tax, etc.

However, there are good accountants out there and some not so good. You need to find an accountant who has an in-depth knowledge of your particular business niche. Whilst you won't find a specialist recruitment accountant, you will be able to find accountants who have worked with recruitment companies in the past.

Finding an accountant comes down to word of mouth and testimonials. You can meet with several and shortlist down to the one who suits your needs best. Of course, you also need to get along with them well and you also need to be able to contact them ever you need an answer on something. There are accountants who work remotely and this may be an issue if you have different time zones, etc. For that reason, perhaps a standard accountant, e.g. an accountant who has standard office hours within a company, is a good option for you.

You can hire an accountant at any stage of your business, but it's best to find a good fit at the start, when you have more time. An accountant can hep you draw up your business plan, for example, if you're struggling to create a plan which you feel is high quality enough to secure you any funding that you need.

An accountant can also provide the following services for you:

- Regular financial reviews, be it bi-yearly, quarterly, or even monthly
- Help with your tax return - this can save a huge amount of time and ensures that your return is submitted without delay and therefore avoiding the risk of a late penalty
- Growth projections and turnover information
- Help with expansion and projections
- Planning out tax over the year

• Managing accounts in general

If you don't have the greatest financial business knowledge, a good quality accountant can take the work off your hands. This frees you up to focus on building your business and the areas of expertise you can specialise in. For instance, you can then focus your time and attention on sourcing out clients and headhunting the best candidates for vacancies.

Of course, you can still do this whilst running your own finances, but you will have less time. If you aren't experienced in financial matters, you will find that you spend longer on this, and because it's such a vital part of a business, you may find that it overtakes the actual day to day running of your recruitment company. In that case, finding the ideal accountant is vital.

You can hire an accountant on several different bases'; you can hire on a part or full time basis or on a retainer. It depends on the level of support you need.

Setting up a Business Bank Account

Your next step is to identify and set up a business bank account that best suits your need. There are countless options here and you need to do more research here to find the best fit.

It is always better to open a business account with a brick and mortar bank. Make sure this is a high profile and reputable bank, who will offer you favourable rates and perhaps even options for lending, now or in the future. You will need to show your business plan for anything like this, so make sure you have it to hand when you visit the branch to set everything up.

It's best to avoid online companies offering business bank accounts. These are fine for basic businesses, but if you want to grow your brand in the future and perhaps accept international payments, when working with overseas companies, you may find that you have problems. Some online banks can't process international payments of this kind and you will then end up out of pocket for work that you've already done.

When opening a business bank account, you will need to show your Companies House registration number, which you will have received at the time of registering your business. You will probably also need to show other details, such as registered address, name of business, number of shareholders, partners, financial information, projected profits, etc. This all helps the bank to find the best business bank account for you. Giving as much information as possible will help them to do this.

Business Insurance Requirements

Unfortunately, we live in a 'no win, no fee' culture and that means your business needs some kind of insurance to protect you against any litigation or other untoward problems. Every business needs insurance, but you need to find the best product for a recruitment company. In that case, you need the same level of insurance as your contractors. This means that any liability, should a problem arise, will be passed along the chain and eliminate your business suffering major losses. They have been times in the past when businesses have unfortunately gone bankrupt due to litigation claims and no insurance. Do not make that mistake.

You might be very committed to running a high quality business and no making mistakes, but you can't cut this chance out completely. Insurance will allow you to do your job to the best of your ability and not be constantly worrying about a small issue turning into a major problem.

As a recruitment company, you should look at the following types of business insurance:

- **Public Liability Insurance** - Protects your business against claims for compensation, should you cause injury or damage to a customer or client
- **Professional Indemnity Insurance** - Covers you for legal costs as a result of an error made by your business and resulting in a claim by a customer or client
- **Employers' Liability Insurance** - By law, you must carry this insurance if you have employees. This means that you are protected as a business should your employees suffer injury or illness as a result of their work
- **Cyber And Data Risk Insurance** - A huge amount of information on different companies and clients will be held in your computer systems and this insurance is therefore vital for you. This protects you against any malicious attacks on your data, such as a virus or loss of information as a result of hacking, etc.

Of course, this goes above and beyond the regular type of insurance you should have on your business property, e.g. fire insurance, etc.

Why You Need to Register For VAT, And do so Quickly

You do not have to register for VAT if your business has a turnover of less than £85,000, however, this number changes regularly so do make sure that you check up to date figures for when you establish your business. However, it's a good idea to register voluntarily even if your business has a turnover of less than this amount.

You might think that it sounds ridiculous to pay VAT when you don't have to but it makes your business look far more established and larger than it is in reality. This is a plus point for attracting clients because they will always search for larger and more established businesses, especially if they are large themselves. By having a registered VAT number, you show that you are credible.

With that in mind, make registering for VAT high up on your list of things to do at the start. You can easily register for VAT with HMRC online and you will receive your dedicated VAT registration number, which can be shown on your website, therefore showing that you are a large, established and credible business.

In the recruitment industry, it's all about impressions. Something as small as this can be a make or break for some clients, so it's worthwhile covering all bases. If all goes according to plan, your turnover would be more than £85,000 in the near future anyway, and you would have to register by law at that point. Save the time when you're busier and do it at the start.

Terms of Business

Before you start trading with your first customer, you need to have your terms of service established and draw up by a solicitor.

Terms of business are also known as 'terms and conditions' or simply 'T&Cs'. This is a document that outlines the contract that you create between your recruitment company and a client or candidate. This gives the outline of your business relationship; it includes what you will do for your customers and what is expected of them. It covers the delivery of services, limitations, and payment regulations, etc.

Whilst you can find templates to build your terms of business online, it's not the best option if you're serious about your business. Whilst this is the free option and saves time, it isn't personalised towards your business and what you're going to be providing. It's far better to have a solicitor draw up your term of business instead. This means they're accurate and they suit your business.

For a recruitment company, it's a good idea to have two separate terms of business documents - one for permanent placements and one for temporary, if you are going to work with temporary vacancies.

Without having accurate terms of business you risk issues throughout trading. This could mean customers not paying you; when you don't have T&Cs in place, or T&Cs which aren't up to scratch, there may be nothing you can do to recoup the cash you've lost.

Make sure that your terms of business are dated, printed, and signed by your clients before you start working for them. You should then give them a copy and keep one for yourself, in their company file. This is therefore a legally binding contract that you can fall back on if there are any issues.

Summary of Business Basic Steps to Take

This chapter has outlined the main steps you need to take when setting up your business. Because we have covered a large amount of ground, let's summarise a list of the things you need to cover before you start moving on to how your business is going to run and the systems you need to set up for work on a day to day basis.

- Create a business plan which covers the basics of your business and the amount you expect to earn over the coming years. This document can then be used to support your application for funding. If you're struggling with this, an accountant can help you.

- Find a name for your business which is legal and available. Also, be sure that it reflects your business and isn't going to cause you any problems in the future if you choose to expand
- Register your company with Companies House, therefore creating a limited company. You will be given a registration number, which you must keep safe
- Find an accountant you gel with, who can help you with the financial actions you need
- Open a business account, steering clear of online companies who may not be able to process overseas payments
- Cover your business insurance requirements as a must do
- Register your business for VAT at the start, even though you do not yet meet the threshold. Display your VAT registration number on your website to show credibility and to make your business look larger than it actually is to customers who are searching for big named recruitment companies
- Ask a solicitor to draw up your terms of business, ensuring that you have two separate versions for permanent and temporary placements.

Once the steps in this checklist have been completed, you can move on to the next stage of setting up your newly established business. The next item you need to tick off your list is compliance with legal guidelines, particularly those pertaining to the recruitment industry.

Chapter 3:

Legal Milestones to Cover

Whilst many of the legal milestones you need to tick off may have already been covered whilst setting up your business, i.e. registering with Companies House and ensuring that your name is legal and available, there are certain specifics which should be highlighted.

By understanding these particular legal requirements that are most pertinent to a recruitment company, you can side-step any potential issues in the future and save yourself time. If you leave these things until a later date, not only are you running the risk of fines and possibly worse, but you're also making more work for yourself.

At this stage, you don't have clients or candidates calling you and you aren't researching companies and headhunting yet. That means you have more time. If you try to cover business basics whilst you're busy firmly establishing your business and concentrating on clients and candidates, you're going to overwhelm yourself.

Ensuring that you stay on the right side of the law is vital in any business, but due to the extremely competitive nature of the recruitment business, one wrong move could easily see you go out of business. Knowing what you need to cover ahead of time, is therefore vital.

The main legal areas you need to place a tick at the side of are:

- **Register for HMRC tax and VAT** - We've already talked about the fact that you don't have to register for VAT unless you earn over a certain threshold, but we now know that it's best to do it at the start, to save time and to give your business an air of credibility.
- **The Data Protection Act** - We won't dwell on this too much right now and we're going to talk in far more detail later on about data protection and specific laws that govern the safety and security of information you hold on people and companies you're dealing with. This is also referred to as GDPR (General Data Protection Regulation). For now, simply understand that you need to cover a quite lengthy list of requirements to ensure that information you hold isn't lost, misused, or accidentally damaged.
- **Agency Worker Regulations** - This is a framework that must be adhered to. It covers the rights of agency workers and ensures that they are treated the same as permanently employed

workers. You may choose to simply specialise in permanent placements, in which case the AWR doesn't apply to you, but if you are going to deal with agency recruitment, this is something you need to familiarise yourself with and ensure that you adhere to.

- **UK Code of Non-Broadcast Advertising, Sales Promotion and Direct Marketing** - Otherwise known as the CAP Code, this covers advertising material and direct marketing communication. This ensures that all marketing material is honest, accurate and not misleading to those reading it. The CAP Code is quite in-depth so it's certainly worth downloading a copy and familiarising yourself with it, to ensure that your advertisements and marketing material all fits the bill and doesn't accidentally overstep the mark. This could land you in serious trouble and could mean fines coming your way.

- **Equality Act 2010** - This is an anti-discrimination act which ensures that everyone is treated equally and fairly. This means that when you're sourcing companies and candidates and choosing the right candidate for a specific vacancy, this should be done on merit, i.e. skills, experience, and that they perform at interview, and not on any other factor. Ensuring that you abide by this is vital, as it an Act covered by law.

- **Health & Safety at Work Act** - Again, this is a requirement by law and ensures that if you have any employees, you provide them with a safe and secure working environment. The Act governs how a workplace should be laid out, risk management, risk assessments, the recording of accidents in the workplace, and protective equipment. It also covers the responsibilities of the employee. You should have a copy of this Act displayed in your workplace, to show compliance. You can be spot-checked by the HSE (Health & Safety Executive) at any time.

- **IR35** - This is a piece of legislation related to tax and it's especially pertinent for a limited company. IR35 allows HMRC to collect extra tax from a contractor who is an employee in name only. For instance, if a contractor is working through a third company or intermediary, making them an employee of their client for all intents and purposes, this piece of legislation becomes pertinent.

The best way to ensure that you cover all the main points you need to cover in relation to the above laws is to do some in-depth research. Most Acts and laws can be read in a simplified version on line, giving you a brief rundown of what they mean, what you need to do in order to comply, and any specific action you need to take for registration or otherwise.

For sure, legal reading might not be the most exciting part of setting up a recruitment company, but it's a step that will ensure you don't run into trouble later on.

Employment Agencies Act 1973

There is one particular legislation that regulates the recruitment industry as a whole - the Employment Agencies Act 1983. As a recruiter, you need to be extremely aware of this Act and understand it completely. Failing to comply with any aspect of this Act could have severe consequences for your business.

Another particular aspect to be aware of is the Recruitment and Employment Confederation, or REC. Many recruiters choose to become a member of the REC. This is to be recommended. Not only does it allow you to have support and advice whenever you need it, without having to try and work out what information is accurate and what isn't, but it also gives your business an air of professionalism and credibility. Clients may be more likely to choose a business that is REC registered than one that isn't.

The REC has many support mechanisms in place to help you understand the Employment Agencies Act 1973 and to ensure that you comply with it. However, let's cover the main aspects of this Act and summarise.

The Employment Agencies Act 1973 specifies that:

- Employment agencies cannot charge candidates (job seekers) for finding them work, either full time, part time, agency or permanent
- Employment agencies can however charge the company they're working with, i.e. the company that has a vacancy they want to be filled. The agency will charge this company a fixed fee, according to the specifications they require
- Agency workers must be given a written contract and their pay mustn't be withheld
- All candidates need to be screened carefully in terms of their suitability for a position, including background checks
- When advertising for vacancies, employment agencies must make it clear that they are an agency

The Act covers a huge range of different areas, but these are the most pertinent to summarise. It's a good idea to sit down and read through this Act as soon as your business is registered and before you start to trade. As a recruiter, you need to understand this Act completely.

We mentioned registering as a member of the REC a little earlier, and if you choose to go ahead with this, you need to adhere to the REC Code of Professional Practice. The existence of this code is what gives your business the credibility aspect –

companies choosing to work with you will know that if you're REC registered, you must adhere to the 10 steps contained within this code. These steps state that you must have respect for:

1. Laws and legislation
2. Honesty and being transparent in all aspects of your practice
3. Working relationships
4. Diversity
5. Safety
6. Professional knowledge
7. Engagement - candidates must know for certain all information regarding a role they're applying for, including hours and pay, etc
8. Accurate and fast payment
9. International recruitment, ensuring it is ethical at all times
10. Privacy and confidentiality standards

Before you begin to put further infrastructure together in terms of how to run your business, spend a considerable amount of time ensuring that you are meeting all laws, legislation and standards required. Again, consider becoming a member of the REC for support and credibility.

Chapter 4:

Creating an Online Presence

Once the basics of setting up your business are complete, you need to turn your attention towards another aspect.

All businesses need an online presence in order to succeed. We live in a digital age and it is no longer possible to do business without using websites, blogs, social media, and online discussion platforms. If you choose to avoid this, you won't get off the ground, it's as simple as that.

Putting together the framework for your online presence needs to be done as you are setting up your business. This will form the basis of how your business works and gives you more scope to reach out to potential candidates. It also gives you a strong platform to attract customers who may be interested in working with you.

The main facets of the online world that you need to incorporate into your recruitment business are:

- A high quality, regularly updated and accurate website

- A blog, not always necessary but very useful
- Social media platforms

Building an online presence takes time but it can pick up speed quite quickly, provided you lay the foundations properly. The first step is to build your website.

How to Create a High Quality Website to Catch Attention

A website is the first type of contact that most companies will have with you. Even if you cold call and ask to speak to management in order to discuss a working arrangement, they will check out your website before they make a decision on whether to work with you or not. Your website is vitally important and there are several boxes you need to tick.

- Needs to look professional and reflect your brand
- Needs to be updated regularly
- Needs to have clear contact details which are completely accurate
- All links need to work at all times - broken links are extremely annoying and show a lack of professionalism
- Needs to have a very clear call to action that is easy for the customer to follow
- Needs to inspire companies to work with you

- Needs to show who you are as a company and perhaps also give a glimpse into the personality of your brand - easy to work with, professional, attention to detail, hard working, etc.

It's a good idea to invest money in your website. This will be the foundation of your work so you need to ensure that it ticks the boxes above. However, there are ways you can find a cost effective website building tool, and then perhaps upgrade as your business picks up speed.

A basic way to get your website started is to use a website builder such as Wix. This is without a doubt one of the easiest to use and it has several attractive themes you can use to create your site. It has a 'drag and drop' feature, so you don't have to know the complicated ins and outs of how to build a specialist website and incorporate code. However, going for the easier option may show your clients that you're not as professional as they would like you to be. In this case, you could think about using WordPress and purchasing a domain name or you could use Square Space. These both offer methods of continuing to build your site as your business starts to attract more custom.

There are many options for building websites and it really comes down to your level of expertise. However, another option is to hire a freelancer to design a high quality and very professional website for you. This is a good choice if you have zero experience of building websites and you want to get the basics right from the get-go. Once the website is built, you can easily maintain it with very little knowledge - the hardest part is building it and from there you can easily pick up the rest with a little practice. A high quality freelancer will also be able to show you how to use the website with very little prior knowledge.

It's certainly worth spending a little of your start-up budget on having your website set up professionally. Remember, your website is how the public sees your business and you will no doubt be judged upon its appearance and ease of use.

You will also need to remember that there are costs attached to renting a website space, e.g. your domain. The aforementioned Wix, WordPress, and Square Space options will charge you very little, perhaps around £10-15 per month, however these aren't the most professional options. Domain and hosting costs per month can reach into the hundreds for the most professional choices, so it's about finding the most cost effective route for you and one which is going to show those visiting your site as much about your company as possible. Again, a freelancer with specialist knowledge of building website will be able to advise you and you can then work together to create the best final product for your business.

Another point to remember is making sure that your website is optimised for mobile use. A huge number of people surf the web during their breaks and when commuting, and that means that more and more of us are using our smartphones or tablets for online browsing. You need both a desktop and mobile optimised site to reach out to the masses, but luckily that's quite easy to do. You simply tick a box when setting up your site to ensure that it can be viewed either as mobile or desktop - do not forget this aspect however as you will be missing out on a huge chunk of visitors and therefore huge chunk of potential revenue.

Once your website is built, you need to maintain it and keep it relevant.

As before, this isn't as difficult as building it. As long as the site was created correctly in the first place, making changes to the site and adding content should be extremely easy.

These are the basics for maintaining your site:

- Check your links on a regular basis and ensure that they take the visitor exactly where it says
- Update any information that has changed and delete any that is no longer necessary or relevant
- Update your content regularly. How regularly that is depends upon your company, but to keep

people engaged and updated with what is going on, once a week should be what you're aiming for
- Post updates on jobs and any relevant news quickly
- Remember to remove any jobs which are no longer open
- Link to your social media platforms (more on that shortly)
- Run a check every so often for viruses or other malware

Your website is the bones of your online presence and it needs to be the shining light in your business and its online approach. In a world where first impressions matter more than ever before, people will judge you and form their impression on what they see on your website. It's very difficult to change a negative first impression and it's far better to impress from the get-go.

Creating a Social Media Presence

The sheer number of people it is possible to reach via social media is astounding. A business that doesn't tap into the power of social media is missing out on a huge number of potential leads.

In the recruitment business, candidates are increasingly using the online world to look for vacancies, but not only regular job boards - social media too. Having a strong social media presence on sites such as Facebook, Twitter and even Instagram means that you can reach out to far more people than you would otherwise be able to do.

Thankfully, it's very easy to set up a business page on the main social media sites and then link back and forth between your pages and your website. Having complete links between all your online presence methods means that you're creating a circle and that circle will ensure that nobody missing anything and nobody forgets anything.

Social media marketing is a little like word of mouth with its power amplified by 10,000. It uses the same basis as regular word of mouth but it's done electronically and shared more times than someone is able to speak. By using social media in the right way, you can easily increase the sheer number of high quality candidates you can recruit for your agency and therefore the vacancies that you have. You can also attract companies to your recruitment business via social media too.

Setting up business pages is quick and easy and from there you need to ensure that you regularly update them. You can add polls, news, interesting vacancies and other pieces of information that you think your followers may find useful. Try to maintain a professional voice to anything you post on social media, as it can be very easy to veer into casual language. Yes, you want to show that you're approachable and easy to work with but you also want to show that you're concerned about business and you care about getting people matched up with the correct jobs, filling vacancies for businesses who need high quality workers.

The word of mouth aspect comes from sharing content. As you gain followers, encourage them to share your content and that creates a cycle of spreading your news. As they share, they share to other people, who continue the sharing cycle. It's a route with huge potential and the more you encourage and update, the more benefits will come your way.

Should You Have a Blog?

Many businesses these days have a blog connected to their website and shared via their social media pages. As a recruitment company, should you do this?

It's a personal choice but it's a good idea to see if it works for you. A blog allows you to connect with your customers on a more personalised level and share information with them connected to recruitment in general. A few ideas of blog posts you could share include:

- How to prepare for an interview
- CV building tips
- Dos and don'ts of interviews or applications
- How to dress to impress

The list goes on.

You can also share important information about the recruitment industry that you think your clients might need to know about or might simply be interested to learn.

Blogs are very easy to set up and you can use the DIY options of Wix or WordPress for this. You could also simply have a separate tab on your website which you use for your blog. It really depends on how compact you want your social media presence to be.

As you post a blog, you would update your website to promote it and you would share it on your social media pages, encouraging your followed to do their sharing work too. This all helps to get the word out about your company, promote your services, and show that you are approachable and want to help.

The downside is that blogging takes up a lot of time and it's something which you need to stay on top of in order for it to work. If you establish a blog and then fail to update it regularly, it shows that you're lacking in professionalism or you simply don't have the time. These could be factors that put a business off working with you. It really can be things that small which work against you.

The ideal rate when updating a blog is weekly at the very least, and if you can, perhaps twice weekly. Of course, you don't want to go too far in the other direction and update too often, as this can look like you have far too much time on your hands! Make your blogs between 600 - 1000 words in length and add in some visual elements, such as images, videos, polls, etc. This will keep people engaged and create a buzz about your blog.

However, that doesn't mean you should blog for the sake of it. If you really don't have anything to post that week, it's far better to wait a week than it is to post something lacking in substance.

The more of a buzz there is, the more followers you will have, and the more followers you have, the more successful your business potential.

You can either write the blog yourself or you can hire a freelancer to write a set number of blogs for you per week. You can either upload them yourself or you can make it part of their contract to upload them for you. Whatever you're both happy with.

The Importance of SEO

Having an online presence as a recruitment company wanting to reach out to an increased number of clients and candidates is one thing, but it has to be an effective one. It's no good having any old presence, it has to be part of a strategy that works. When that strategy isn't working or its showing signs of needing change, you adjust and move forwards once more. Every single business on the planet, recruitment or otherwise, needs to have a digital marketing strategy in place, including all of the points we've talked about in this chapter so far. What we haven't talked about yet is perhaps the most important aspect - SEO.

SEO stands for Search Engine Optimisation.

When a customer or client searches for recruitment companies on a search engine, such as Google, a huge list will come up. It's a common truth that nobody really looks past the second page of search results, and it's quite uncommon for them to go past the first one. So, if you're not optimising your content to make sure that you're on that first page, you're going to miss out and you're practically handing business to your competitors who have more of a grip on what SEO is.

Learning SEO isn't difficult but again, you can choose to outsource your content writing and website design to a freelancer who has an in-depth knowledge of SEO. You're then giving yourself the best possible chance at being noticed.

It really comes down to researching keywords that are regularly searched for and then seamlessly and carefully inserting these into your content. This has to be done strategically, e.g. in the title, in at least one subheading in your content, and evenly throughout the page. It cannot however be done too much, because Google will flag this up as unfair play and you may be blacklisted as a result. That's a disaster in terms of digital marketing.

Ensuring that your website pages and the content you use, e.g. social media pages and blog posts, are all SEO'd means that you are far more likely to rank higher up on the search engine results page and as a result, you're more likely to be clicked on. From there, the impressive nature of your website will ensure that customers choose you to work with, rather than clicking off your page and going to one of your competitors instead.

Customer Reviews/Testimonials And How They Help You

Recruitment is very people-orientated. It's a service you give to people to help them find a job that challenges them and which they enjoy. From a client's point of view, it's a service you give to help them find the best talent for their available vacancies. With that in mind, having testimonials and reviews from people you've helped in the past will certainly go a long way towards boosting the power your website holds.

People believe reviews.

If you think about when you're booking a hotel for an upcoming holiday, you probably head over to TripAdvisor and take those reviews into account when it comes to making your final choice. Some reviews will be good, some bad, some indifferent, but they help to inform your choice.

Having a section with customer reviews on your website helps to build trust and trust is one of the most important marketing strategies you can have. People want to know that when they work with you, they're getting exactly what you promise and that the quality is high.

However, having a review section needs to be designed carefully. Firstly, make sure they're real reviews and don't make them up. People can spot this a mile away and it erodes trust and credibility very quickly. Also, don't have every single review a glowing gushing and five star affair. Yes, they need to be impressive and positive, but you shouldn't have people shouting from the rooftops on every single review - no business is perfect.

Simply choose a range of reviews that show the best side of your business and have a section for people to leave their reviews. This shows that you have nothing to hide, that you want to improve your service from the comments that customers leave behind, and impresses people who are looking to make the final decision on whether to work with you or not.

Of course, you should set reviews to manual, so you can review them before they're posted on your website. This stops any potentially damaging remarks, and you can act as a moderator before accepting the comment to be posted on your site. This isn't censorship, it's about ensuring that your site isn't the victim of a damaging attempt to undermine your reputation. This can happen in some cases by not only unhappy customers but also by random people - not everyone out there is honest and the Internet is a hotbed of viruses, phishing scams, and all manner of other malicious outlets.

Whilst creating a strong online presence might seem like a huge mountain to climb, and we've covered a huge amount of information in this chapter, it's vital that you take it all in, digest it, and work on it carefully. For a recruitment company in particular the online world is imperative. This is the face of your business, and it helps you to reach out to far more people than would ever be possible in a manual way.

Chapter 5:

The Importance of GDPR And Your Responsibilities

A little earlier in the book, we talked about the Data Protection Act and we touched upon something called GDRP. In this chapter, we're going to do a deep dive into what both of these elements mean for a recruitment company, what your responsibilities are, and how to ensure that you do everything you're meant to do.

Over the last few years, there has been a huge push to ensure that information held on businesses and individuals is kept safe and secure. This is mostly down to the increasing amount of digital storage we use. A few decades ago we used to hold information manually, in locked, fire-proofed filing cabinets. These weren't 100% secure by any means but they had safeguards in place. These days, everything is held on a computer and there is an increased risk of theft, loss, or damage as a result.

There are two main pieces of legislation you need to bear in mind if you hold any information on an individual - the Data Protection Act 1998 and General Data Protection Regulation (GDPR). In this chapter, we'll explore both, but let's start with the oldest one first.

The Data Protection Act 1998

The Data Protection Act 1998 was recently updated in 2018 to include GDPR, however the basic principles remain the same and the legislation is still enshrined within UK law. As a result, your recruitment company must adhere to all parts of the Act. Failure to do so may result in severe consequences for your business.

The Data Protection Act protects any personal information that is stored ether manually or digitally by a company, related to another company or an individual. In this case, that would cover your clients (the businesses you are trying to recruit for) and the candidates you're trying to find work for.

The Act covers the collection, organisation, storage, use, communication, combination restriction and the destruction of this information. As a result, you must follow guidelines at all times when using information, storing it, destroying it, and for any other use. The overall aim is to ensure that information is used in a legal way, a fair way, and in a transparent way.

Under the Data Protection Act you must ensure that information you hold is:

- Used only for the specified purpose
- Use in a lawful way, a fair way, and a completely transparent way
- Used in a way which is limited to what is relevant and necessary only
- Accurate and updated to be up to date, if necessary
- Kept only for the length of time required
- Only handled by those who need to use it, and protected against viewing by anyone who doesn't need to see it
- Protected against loss, theft, or unauthorised access
- Destroyed in a careful and necessary way

These are called Data Protection Principles and they cover all information held. However, there is more in-depth protection for information which is considered to be particularly sensitive, such as ethnicity, race, religious beliefs, health and genetics, sexual orientation, etc. There are other safeguards in place for anything which relates to criminal history.

As a recruitment company, you should not hold any information on an individual which isn't necessary for the role. For instance, you shouldn't ask someone their sexual orientation and hold that information because it has no bearing on jobs they may or may not be suitable for. This should only come down to their skills and experience and holding irrelevant information, particularly sensitive information, will land you in breach of Data Protection rules.

Under the Data Protection Act, individuals are able to request access to the information you hold on them at any time. This enables people to find out how their data is used and to ensure that data is accurate and up to date. They can also request for specific data to be erased or make a complaint about how their data is used.

In order to request this, the individual must write to the organisation and make a request under the Data Protection Act. Within one month maximum, the company must reply and provide the individual with a copy of the information that is held on them. If there is a delay, this must be for a very valid reason and the individual must be informed within one month of the delay. The information must therefore take no longer than two months to be supplied to the individual.

There are certain situations in which a company can refuse the request, but these circumstances aren't likely to be encountered by a recruitment company.

These types of situations usually revolve around national security or crime problems.

As the owner of any business, it is vital to understand and adhere to the Data Protection Act. As the owner of a recruitment company, you will have access to a large amount of data on your candidates and clients and it's vital that you ensure everything you hold is necessary, safe, secure, and only accessed by those who need to use it for their role within the company.

There are also rules as to how long you can keep this information on record. In terms of recruitment, you can hold this information for as long as you need to in order to complete the function, i.e. you would hold information on a candidate for as long as it takes you to find them a job, or for as long as they choose to work with you as a recruiter. You would hold information on a client, e.g. a company you were recruitment for, for as long as you have them on your books and they require your services. After this time, you would have to destroy this information in a sensitive and safe way.

Whilst looking into Data Protection you will also come across GDPR. This is a more recent development and an update on the older Data Protection laws. GDPR stands for General Data Protection Regulation and came into play in 2018.

What is GDPR And Why is it Important?

GDPR is an EU-wide regulation. Post-Brexit this won't cover sole UK transactions but if you are recruiting international candidates, working with companies in EU countries or you're processing information from someone who is from an EU country, you will need to ensure that you're adhering to these guidelines. As a result, you should familiarise yourself very carefully indeed. Again, any company that fails to adhere to these guidelines will find themselves in deep trouble, with severe financial consequences.

GDPR has six principles, which are very similar to the older Data Protection Act, but which are slightly updated for the modern day. These include:

1. Lawful use, fair use, and transparent use of data
2. Limited only to the purpose for which the data is required
3. Minimising data, e.g. only holding the information you really need and nothing more
4. Ensuring data is accurate and up to date wherever necessary
5. Stored in a secure manner
6. Used only by those who need access and confidentiality is maintained

The overall rules of GDPR are quite lengthy, so it is important that as the owner of a recruitment company you know the summarised responsibilities you hold and you adhere to them at all times. The main points to remember are:

• GDPR allows individuals and companies to know what information is held about them and what it is being used for
• GDPR allows individuals and companies to know if their data is being shared with other companies or agencies
• GDPR allows individuals and companies to access the data you hold (as with the Data Protection Act) and transport it elsewhere if they choose - this is known as 'data portability'
• In some cases, GDPR allows individuals and companies to request that their data is permanently erased
• Certain companies are required to have a Data Protection Officer nominated within their workforce, who is responsible for handling requests to view data and any other issues related to the Act. This person is also responsible for ensuring that GDPR is implemented
• GDPR states that companies who experience data breaches must inform those affected within 72 hours of the breach occurring

The reason this is all so pertinent to you as a recruitment company is because you are going to hold a lot of relevant information on your candidates and your clients. Regularly reviewing your records and destroying information that is no longer required should be something you do on a regular and cyclical basis.

The consequences of breaking GDPR, in particular, are severe. In some cases, this can be a warning, if the breach is minor and it is the first offence. However, there can also be very large fines. The most serious breaches of GDPR rules can create a major headache for business owners, with fines that can go up to 20 million Euros, or 4% of the total revenue of that company. The GDPR fine will, therefore, opt for the highest of those two choices.

The information you hold as a recruitment company will not be manual. Gone are the days when you had paper-based records and held them in a filing cabinet. If you choose to go down that route, you're seriously outdated and need to understand how technology runs the recruitment world. In our next section, we're going to talk about the technical side of recruitment. Let's first start with security.

Website Security Concerns

In order to adhere to Data Protection legislation of all kinds, you have to make sure that your website is secure. This ensures that hackers and all other kinds of security risks can't pose a threat to the information you hold in your systems.

It's far more likely that you will receive applications and CVs online these days, via email or uploaded to your secure site, than you will receive paper versions. Of course, you may still receive some, but the online version is without a doubt the preferred route for most applicants nowadays. By offering this service you're ensuring that you're opening up your recruitment business for the maximum number of candidates you can reach, whilst also streamlining the process of receiving applications for vacancies.

Whilst this is a great way to make life easier when it comes to receiving information from people, it also means that you need to double up your efforts to ensure that your site is safe and secure. This is required of you via the Data Protection Act and GDPR.

Let's look at the steps you need to take to ensure that your website is secure.

- **Secure your website with SSL (Secure Sockets Layer certificate)** - GDPR doesn't specify that you need SSL, but the fact that you're going to be receiving and holding information on individuals and companies means that you need it. This will help to make your site GDPR compliant. SSL basically encrypts information so that it can't be stolen or read by malicious third parties.
- **Regularly scan your website** - You should purchase a high quality antivirus and anti-malware package and run regular scans to check that nothing untoward is happening with your website and causing information to be stolen and perhaps distributed elsewhere. Many high quality software packages in this niche will run scheduled checks and flag up any issues, so you should ensure you set this up and that way you won't forget.
- **Change your passwords regularly** - You need very strong passwords that can't be cracked and you need to change them regularly. It goes without saying that you should never write passwords down or allow anyone else to have knowledge of them.
- **Make sure that you update the software on a regular basis** - Again, most software packages will have automatic or scheduled updates, but you should always check that you're using the most up to date version of any packages you regularly use. This means your antivirus and anti-malware

software will run in tandem and secure you against any risks.

- **Never reply to unknown emails** - There are many scammers out there who will send emails and try and entice you to open an attachment or click on a link. If you don't know the sender of an email and you're not confident what it's about, do not open it and don't click on it. These are scams which either contain viruses or trick you into giving out information that then allows a hacker to access sensitive information.

Aside from securing your website you also need to run regular backups. This means that information you hold is kept safe against any issues, such as computer or server crashes, etc. The repercussions of losing all the information you hold on clients and candidates are extremely far-reaching and could put you out of business in the worst case scenario. Backing up means that you're insuring yourself against this happening and helping to cover Data Protection and GDPR regulations, by ensuring everything is safe and secured.

You might be wondering about emails and this is also something to consider in terms of keeping any information confidential and safe. You may receive applications and CVs also via email, and in that case, you have a responsibility to ensure that this information is dealt with in the same sensitive way as the information you receive via your website.

Encrypted emails are a good route, but not everyone uses these. Sites such as Tutanota use end to end encryption and inform the recipient that they have received an encrypted email, which they need a password to be able to open. This is particularly useful if you are sending any applicant information to a client, prior to the interview. All that needs to be done is the client also registers for a free Tutanota account and you can safely transfer information without worrying about it falling into the wrong hands or being used maliciously.

Obviously, there are several other encrypted email software packages you can use and you should look around and find the best one for you.

For regular emails you will receive from candidates, perhaps with their personal information on, you should ensure that you have a password on your email account that you don't share it, you don't write it down, and you change it regularly. Once you receive an email such as this, transfer the information into your confidential data system (more on that shortly), and delete the email both out of your inbox and your trash box. Never keep emails as they can easily be hacked and you will then be in breach of Data Protection and GDPR.

Organising Yourself With a Compliant CRM System

The information you hold on your customers and especially your candidates needs to be kept somewhere safe, but ideally also somewhere you can retrieve the details you need without having to look through every file manually, on screen. In that case, you need a GDPR compliant and high quality CRM system.

A Customer Relationship Management (CRM) system not only keeps information secure and safe, but it also helps to organise your workload and saves a huge amount of time in the process. Put simply, a good quality CRM helps to protect, organise and manage customer information. You can pull out records with ease, simply by asking for what you need and you can keep a record of any communications or other details that you want to note down. You can also keep a simple track of which candidates have applied for which vacancies, and you can organise the candidates in your database according to skills and experience.

However, there are countless CRM systems out there and you need to be sure that you're choosing the best one for you.

A few good quality options to think about include Bullhorn, Voyager, and Vincere. Make sure that you opt for a CRM with good quality support, just in case you encounter any software problems and you need them sorted out quickly.

There are three main types of CRM, including desktop systems that run on just one computer, i.e. only one computer has access to it, a server-based system that keeps all your information securely on a server and can be installed on several PCs or laptops, or a Cloud-based system which can be accessed anywhere, on any device, with just the necessary log in details.

There are certain security and cost implications to consider here.

Obviously having a desktop system may seem like the cheapest version, but it does limit how many people can access this, e.g. if you have several employees who all need access to the system during their working day. There is also the issue of if something goes wrong with that particular PC, and that means you're also locked out of your CRM until the issue is resolved - if it can be. In many ways, the desktop top is the dated way to run a CRM but it's still an option that you can weigh up.

A server-baed system runs on your own internal IT security system and you will need to spend money on paying for the system and installing it. Updates may be difficult and expensive once more, and In some ways, mobile use can be difficult depending upon the CRM product itself. Despite that sounding quite negative, there are some very high quality server-based CRM systems to consider, so it's not something to discount immediately.

These days however, many companies choose to use Cloud-based CRM systems. These are normally cheaper to purchase and you'll pay a minimal monthly subscription fee to keep your membership up and running. You don't have to think about security as it is included in the product, as part of the ongoing fee you pay. Any updates are also included and you can connect to your CRM system anywhere, on the go, simply by logging in on any device.

The CRM you opt for is a personal choice, so be sure to shop around and explore your choices before deciding. It's best to stick with your first choice, as transferring information between CRMs can be laborious and difficult.

Spend some time getting to know your CRM before you start sourcing clients and candidates. This will give you an idea of exactly what your CRM can do and how it works. This saves time and allows you to get the most out of it from the start.

Summing up Part 1

We've now reached the end of our first part, and now you have all the basic information you need to set up your recruitment company.

At first, the whole endeavour may have seemed like a mountain to climb, but by this point, things should certainly seem a lot clearer. Take each section at a time and work through it in a checklist fashion. By ensuring that you take the time to cover the foundations of your business set up, you'll find everything else is far easier and smoother as a result.

We have already summed up our first section on business basics, so if you remain unsure of any points you need to follow, go back and read the first couple of chapters once more. Make sure you cover these basic points to set up your business and register it properly.

Your website is the next point you need to concentrate on. This may be something you choose to outsource to a freelancer and whilst it will cost you some of your start up budget, it's a good idea to do this if you have no prior experience or interest in setting up websites. Equally, if you don't have a natural flair for writing or you simply don't think you're going to have the time, you can outsource your blogging and social media marketing tasks to a freelance writer and pay them per month for a set number of posts. This is beneficial because a high quality content writer will also have extensive knowledge of SEO, helping to send more visitors your way and hopefully converting into customers and clients.

Your online presence is the public face of your recruitment company, so you should not scrimp on the amount of time you spend in this section. Make sure that the online presence you build is solid and considerable, honest and engaging. By doing this, you will not only attract more clients but you'll gain a greater database of candidate details too.

We've also spent a considerable amount of time in this section talking about the protection and security of data. The Data Protection Act and GDPR is something you need to understand and know about inside out in terms of your responsibilities. Failing to do this can land you in extremely hot water and cause major problems for your business. Make sure your website is GDPR compliant and have procedures in place to maintain the security of any information you receive and store.

The final point is to find a high quality and easy to use CRM, or Customer Relationship Management system. Browse your choices and find one which seems naturally easy to you and one which gives you a large amount of support, should something go wrong with the system itself. There are many different types and options, and you should choose carefully to ensure that you don't end up having to transfer all your information over to another system in the near future. Get the choice right from the start and you'll save time and money.

We've now completed our first section on how to set up a recruitment company. Our second section will focus on how to run a successful recruitment company, giving you tips on how to manage your workload and make life infinitely easier as a result.

PART 2

RUNNING A SUCCESSFUL
RECRUITMENT COMPANY

Chapter 1:

What Are Your Aims?

If you want to run a successful recruitment company, you need to know what you want to work towards. This is the same with anything in life - goals and aims keep you on track and stop you from wandering towards a path that is less desirable or less successful.

Every single business needs to have aims to work towards, but this is perhaps even more important when running a recruitment company. This is because there are many metrics you can use to measure how well you're doing and identify areas you for improvement. Some industries don't have metrics they can measure success against, so the fact that in recruitment you have these at your disposal means you should use them!

In our last part we laid out the foundations to set up your business but now it's time to kickstart the action. The first step is to work out what you want to achieve in the first year, the second year, and up to five years. Whilst there may be situations to overcome that knock your aims back a few months, the key is to readjust and stay on target.

Setting Your First Year Targets

The first year is the most important for a recruitment company, because whilst you're new, you have the chance to really make an impact. After the first year, the aim should be to have gained back any costs incurred in setting up your business and to have made a good profit. The first year is also about building reputation and working relationships.

As you will come to realise, reputation is everything in the recruitment industry and it can easily be damaged. For that reason, ensuring that you make careful and measured decisions is vital.

Having first year targets in place means that you can review these quarterly and perhaps tweak your approach if you find that you're not quite where you should be just yet.

The main targets to focus on during your first year include:

• **Sales** - How many sales do you want to have achieved by the end of your first year? This will be the number of successful contracts with clients that have yielded a fee paid to you.

- **Number of permanent contracts** - This is the number of candidates you have successfully placed within a vacancy advertised as permanent.
- **Number of temporary contracts** - Similarly, this is the number of candidates you have successfully placed within a vacancy advertised as temporary. If you're not going to specialise in temporary contracts then obviously forget this particular target.
- **Average fee charged** - In the coming chapters we are going to talk in more detail about the fees you will charge your clients. remember, you don't charge your candidates but you will charge the companies who have vacancies they want to fill. The fee you charge depends upon their requirements, and an average over the course of the first year will give you an idea of whether you have scope to increase your prices, or whether you should stick with what you have.
- **Client referrals** - How many clients came to you via your website, your social media platforms, cold calling, etc? Identify a rate for each channel and identify whether extra work needs to be done in one particular area versus another.
- **Candidate referrals** - As above, identify where your candidates came to you from and work out whether extra work needs to be done.
- **Client retention** - The number of clients you won and then retained on your books for future vacancies. This is a key 'word of mouth' marketing strategy done correctly!

These are key metrics you can use to measure success and to identify areas of improvement but they're also areas you can use to estimate targets. Have a rough number at the side of each of the above and assess every quarter whether you're close to hitting that target or not.

Aside from this, you should also have monthly monitoring on:

- **Cost per hire** - How much of your budget does it cost to place a candidate within a vacancy? Keeping an eye on this gives you information on where money can be saved.
- **Retention rate** - How many of your vacancies are successful over the long-term? If you place a candidate within a vacancy and they turn out to be unfit for the job and leave after a few weeks, this is going to damage your reputation. Make sure that you have a high retention rate to keep your clients happy.
- **Time to hire** - How long does it take to fill a vacancy? Obviously, this shouldn't be super-quick, because you don't have the time to ensure quality, but it shouldn't be too long either. Work at reducing your time to hire in a reasonable manner.

Checking these metrics on a monthly basis will show you where money can be saved and also where time can be saved too.

The Importance of Goals

Setting out your first year objectives gives you the motivation to continue when things may be difficult. During the first year of any business, you learn how things work, what doesn't work, and how to tweak things to bring you greater success. You will make mistakes during this first year, but it's about minimising their impact and ensuring that you can overcome them and also learn from them too.

Goals provide you with a measure to work towards, motivation and they also help you to understand how well you're actually doing. It's easy to assume that things are going well business-wise, but it's possible that it's a smokescreen. There are good clients and there are not so good ones, and by focusing on all clients, you're perhaps wasting time and energy. It's far better to focus on the clients who provide you with reliable work, those who pay on time and give good reviews to help you attract more clients in the future.

Of course, that doesn't mean you shouldn't pay equal attention to clients who may be a little more demand or difficult, but if a client is constantly paying late, if they're changing their requirements constantly and not allowing you to provide them with the best possible service, you have to question whether that is time well spent or not. Remember, time is money.

Aside from the first year objectives above, you should have your own personal business goals in place. These are the things you want to achieve and some of them will be already enshrined in your business plan.

Within the first year, what do you want to have achieved within your recruitment company? Then ask yourself where you would like your company to be in five years' time. Do you have any growth ideas that you can revisit at a later date? Dreaming big when starting a company isn't a waste of time or having 'pie in the sky' ideas, it's a great way to motivate you to keep going and pushing yourself to achieve those goals and aims.

A business without goals will simply drift. They may make a profit and they may tick along nicely, but they won't grow and they won't increase those profits or take more of the market share as a result of their efforts. Having goals and aims will allow you to do this.

Before you start to set your pricing structure before you attempt to reach out to clients and candidates, and before you even start to become completely au fait with your new CMS, make sure that you know exactly what you're trying to achieve.

Chapter 2:

Set Your Fees Competitively

Your fees may or may not be included in your business plan, but it's vital either way to ensure that you set these fees fairly and competitively if you want your recruitment company to succeed.

You do not charge fees to the candidates you source. The talent that you identify for vacancies is a free service that you provide, however, you recoup that time, effort and money back in the fees you charge to the clients you have on your books, i.e. the companies who have vacancies that need to be filled, or the future vacancies you identify for them.

Your pricing structure will depend upon many different variables but the difference between permanent and temporary employees is probably the biggest. Not all recruitment companies choose to advertise for temporary vacancies, but by not offering this service, you may be missing out on a large share of the market. Clients regularly need both temporary and permanent staff for various different vacancies, and a business is not going to work with you for their permanent requirements and another recruitment company for their temporary needs. They're far more likely to regularly stick with a company that offers both services. That needs to be you.

It's not possible to tell you what your rates should be, but we can give averages that you can work with. There are many different variables that will inform what you charge a client, and it could also come down to geographical location - vacancies in large capital cities will usually have higher salaries and therefore the cost of your services will need to be reflected within that. The fee may also be higher for vacancies which are quite difficult to fill, e.g. they're very specialised or niche, and require in-depth research to find the best talent fit for the job.

Rates For Permanent Placements

An average of between 15-20% of the role's final annual salary is the general rate charged for permanent vacancies. This is a one off fee you charge to the client at the end of your services, i.e. once the role is filled. If a role is extremely niche and will prove to be difficult to find the best candidate, you can increase your fee, perhaps up to 25% of the annual salary.

There are two main ways a company may use your services. They may use more than one recruitment company and then whichever company's candidate is successful in being recruited will receive the fee, or you can be employed by the client exclusively, and your recruitment company is solely responsible for filling their vacancies. In this type of situation, you may be able to increase your rates, perhaps up to 30% or even 50% in extremely specialised niches.

Some clients may insist on a rebate of your fees if the candidate is successfully recruited to the post but leaves within a certain amount of time. This is best avoided, so obviously sourcing out the highest quality talent for a role is necessary to avoid this type of situation. This not only loses time and money but also damages your reputation.

Rates For Temporary Placements

Setting the fee for a temporary employee is not as straightforward as with a permanent employee, which is perhaps why some recruitment companies choose not to work with temporary placements.

When setting your pricing structure for temporary vacancies you will need to think about the salary the employee will receive, holiday pay, their National Insurance contributions the amount of profit that you're looking to make. Temporary employee vacancy fees are often therefore decided on a case by case basis, to ensure that the effort is worth the final profit margin received.

With temporary employees, the costs of recruiting the candidate are paid for by the recruitment company themselves and they are then billed to the client and recouped back. As an average amount however, 15% of the equivalent salary or daily rate is often the fee charged by a recruitment company in this case.

At the start of your recruitment journey however, it's a good idea to be competitive and flexible with your pricing. Whilst you shouldn't drop your prices to the point where you're not making any profit, you should think about the fact that you're untried and untested in the eyes of a client. This means that if your prices are lower, they may be more likely to work with you and therefore build up a working relationship over time, than go with a company with an established reputation.

You need to weigh up the work versus the profit margin you're aiming for when setting a fee to charge to clients. However, do some market research into your local area or your desired niche and find out what your competitors are charging. Check out both new recruitment company pricing structures and established ones, and come up with a structure of your own which is both attractive to clients but also enough to give you a profit you can work with.

As you become more established and you have regular working relationships with clients, you can slowly start to increase your fees to reflect your experience.

Create a Regular Invoicing Schedule

The fact that you are going to bill your clients for the work done at the end of the process, i.e. when a candidate has been successfully recruited into a position, means that there is a risk of non-payment. Your terms of business need to have been signed, printed, dated and kept by both you and the client in order to have that legally binding contract in place.

Whilst most clients will happily pay their invoices on time, there will always be difficulties experienced in some cases. Unfortunately, large businesses don't place importance upon paying invoices the moment they land on their desks, because they have so many other things to focus on too. You need to have a schedule in place which allows you to automatically bill your clients, and then a reminder to chase up after a set amount of time. This will reduce the chances of you being paid late or experiencing difficulties getting paid in the first place.

It's important to be clear about pricing and payment dates when agreeing to work with a client.

Your terms of business will state this, but it's useful to point it out and have a separate document stating the fee and the amount of time this should be paid within. You can attach this to your terms of business and this gives you peace of mind and extra protection against non-payers or difficult payers.

For specialist vacancies, the fee a recruitment company can earn can be large. For instance, if you're charging a flat 25% rate for a difficult to recruit to position, and the annual salary is £45,000 per year, you will receive £11,250. Having to chase that large amount isn't something you want to have to do, as it will cut into the time you have available to focus on other clients.

Some CMS software will send invoices for you and will also send reminders after a set amount of time. This is a feature to look for when shopping around for the best CMS for you, but if your particular choice doesn't have this feature, put into a place a manual system which flags up on your calendar, so an excessive amount of time doesn't pass before payment is received.

Covering Your Tax Requirements

In our first part, we mentioned that you need to enlist the help of a quality accountant to make life easier for you and to save time. However, when you are paid your fee from a successful contract with a client, you need to remember that you're going to need to pay your taxes at the end of the year!

It's far better to do this on a rolling basis, i.e. you save the correct amount of tax from each contract and place it in a separate account. This means that when your tax return is due, the full amount is there, ready to be paid.

This is a mistake that many companies make. They simply assume that they can pay their tax bill at the end of the year, but they don't save enough from each contract. As a result, they're left with a huge bill to pay and not enough cash to cover it.

HMRC tax rates change slightly for each tax year, so be sure to check accurate figures before setting aside the right amount you need. However, current rates stand at 20% of your yearly earnings if your earnings are between £12,501 to £50,000 (basic rate), and 40% of your yearly earnings if your earnings are between £50,001 to £150,000. The higher rate of 45% applies to earnings of over £150,000.

If you choose not to work with an accountant, this is something you need to bear in mind as a priority, however, choosing to do your own accounts is both time consuming and risky if you don't have in-depth knowledge of business finances and tax regulations. For that reason, make sure that you liaise regularly with your accountant and ensure that tax requirements and VAT are covered as you go along, and not left until the end of the year when you might find yourself struggling to cover a large HMRC bill.

A successful recruitment company is streamlined and has every eventuality taken into account to make life easier - tax included.

Creating Quality Advertisements

When advertising a vacancy, you need to ensure that you create a high quality and eye-catching advertisement. This will ensure that you attract the best talent and encourage them to apply to the vacancy.

By law, you need to mention on the advertisement in clear terms that you are a recruitment agency acting on behalf of a specific company. This cannot be missed out otherwise you will find yourself breaching legal legislation, as mentioned in the first part of the book.

Of course, advertisements cost money and you need to ensure that you factor the cost of this into the fees you charge to your clients. There are however some very easy ways to ensure that you attract the right candidates to a vacancy via your advertisement.

- **Make your adverts stand out** - Think about the layout and make sure that the design is in keeping with the role itself. You should also include a hook at the start of the advert, which grabs the attention and makes the right kind of potential candidate continue reading.
- **Include as much information as possible, without making it too 'wordy'** - Advertisements are, by nature, quite snappy and short, but you should try and include the most important basics of the role. This ensures that potential candidates know as much as possible about the role they may apply for. You would obviously give more information, e.g. job description and person specification, on your website.
- **Make sure all details are accurate** - Never place false or inaccurate information on any of your advertisements as this is misleading and could also land you in hot water with relevant legislation.
- **Give a clear call to action and contact details** - Make sure that what to do next is clear, e.g. follow this link and complete an application form, send CV and covering letter to a specific email or upload to your website. You should also have clear contact details for people to call or email if they have any further questions they want to ask before applying.

- **Share your advertisements in the relevant places**
  - Make sure that you upload the advertisement to your website, to your newsletter emailed out to candidates on your database, share it on your social media platforms, and also send a copy out to relevant trade magazines and sites. Again, make sure it is clear on the advertisement that you are a recruitment agency.

Covering the costs of your recruitment efforts is vital if you want to make sure that you achieve a good enough profit from each client. More and more recruitment companies are moving towards flat fees, which makes it easier for the client to understand helps them to plan their own finances accordingly. This is something you can look towards as you start to work with various clients and you understand the amount of work and costs that go into each placement. Once you understand this, set out a flat guide with percentages for each type of role; obviously with more specialised roles commanding a higher flat fee percentage.

Being competitive against your rivals will also help you to be the one clients choose, rather than regularly missing out on work that could potentially have a high profit margin attached to it.

Chapter 3:

Building Strong Working Relationships

At the heart of every successful recruitment company is the strength of its working relationships.

You are working within an industry that is extremely people-focused and that means you need to build trust with every single client and candidate you sign up to your agency. Sometimes it can be as easy being misunderstood by a client cause them to sign with one of your competitors, rather than with you.

Strong working relationships hinge on:

- Trust
- Communication
- Commitment
- Integrity
- A common goal

In our next section, we're going to talk at length about trust and how this is one of the most important parts of building a strong working relationship with your clients and also with your candidates.

Some companies place more importance on their clients than their candidates but that's a mistake. Both are equally important and your recruitment company would not exist without either one. Yes, you need big clients to sign with you because you charge them a fee and that is where your revenue comes from. However, without high quality talent, i.e. your candidates, you're not going to have clients signing up with you either.

The fact that you cannot charge a fee to candidates should not mean that you give them a lesser service than your clients. By ensuring that your candidates are high quality, they understand the job brief that they're applying for and that you help them to be prepared for interviews and with CV building, you're going to ensure that they're placed in a job which suits them best. As a result, they'll stay in that job, and you won't have your recruitment reputation damaged because you chose a sub-standard candidate for a client's vacancy.

You are providing a service to both, and whilst it's an opposite-facing service, it's one that needs to be equal in terms of time and attention.

This means that you need to ensure high quality communication at all times. Building strong working relationships basically means that you feel able to ask questions and the same goes for them. This helps you to work together better, and reach the common goal that you both have, i.e. finding the right person for the vacancy.

Integrity comes down to not always going for the easy option, and instead going for the best outcome option. You might have several candidates on your books who could do a perfectly fine job, but you know about a high quality talent who would perform within this role to stratospheric levels. Yes, you could opt for the easier choice and recruit one of your existing candidates, or you could try and headhunt the person who you know would be the best person for the role. It's the harder option, but you're acting with integrity for your client, because it's the best choice for them.

Remember, your job as a recruiter is to find the best person for a job, and to help your candidates find jobs which allow them to fulfil their potential.

The Importance of Trust

Many companies have internal HR departments and most of the time they deal with recruitment. However, HR departments deal with all manner of other issues too, from organisational policies to disciplinary issues. That means that their entire focus is not on the recruitment side of things. That is your 'in' when trying to find clients to sign up to your agency. Your USP (Unique Selling Point) here is that you can focus completely upon finding the best person for the job, therefore increasing the company's productivity and success in the future.

However, all of this hinges upon the client trusting you to do the job. They are not going to pay a rather sizeable fee to an agency when they can ask their HR department to do it for free, unless they can be sure that you are going to deliver results that far exceed those their internal workers could achieve.

There are many ways to build trust, including:

- Regular and effective communication
- Doing exactly what you say you're going to do
- Not making false promises
- Checking in with your client/candidates regularly
- Asking questions and not simply telling them what to do
- Showing your results to back up your claims
- Keeping them informed every step of the way

It really comes down to treating your clients and your candidates with respect and working together to reach your common goal. Without trust, you will not get very far in an industry which relies so heavily on human interaction. It is also very easy to damage trust and in that case, damage limitation needs to kick into play extremely quickly.

If a customer has a complaint, or they're not happy with an aspect of the service, you should call them and arrange a meeting quickly. By doing this, you're showing them that you care about how they feel and that you want to rectify whatever is causing the problem. Swift action at this point can help to side-step damaging your working relationship and can also stop damaging word of mouth negative remarks.

Never underestimate the power of word of mouth in today's world. Several years ago this would have been done by people actually talking to one another and reporting back either negativity or positively about a service. These days this news can carry ten times further, due to social media and the fact that we're all far more connected than we have ever been before.

This means that one misunderstanding, if not rectified quickly, could be passed from company to company, and that means you're losing business. Candidates may also speak to one another and choose not to sign with your company as a result of their friend or family member's experience with you.

For that reason, ensure that you treat people well, that you maintain communication and that you focus on trust as a first port of call. Recruitment may be digitalised and complicated in many ways, but the basics of treating people with respect are more important than anything else.

Finding Clients and Candidates

There are many different ways you can reach out to potential clients and candidates. As you start to run your recruitment business you'll need to use several of them and cast your net wide. As time goes on, you can specialise a little more.

Cold calling clients is one of the best ways to identify clients who may want to work with you. You can check online job boards and perhaps call the companies concerned, offering to take over their recruitment efforts. Or, you can do some research of your own and identity the types of companies you would like to work with. Then, call and ask to speak to a member of their management.

Of course, you will need to sell your services and that means having notes written down beforehand and perhaps a presentation or package that you can send over to them. You would then schedule a time to call them back to chase up on the lead.

Gathering referrals and word of mouth is also a good way to identify clients, but also candidates too. You can easily keep your ear to the ground and find out about high quality talent who you may want to sign up to your agency, or encourage to apply for a specific vacancy that you're working with currently.

However, you should never overlook the power of social media. LinkedIn is a hotbed of prospective candidates and by browsing those who may be suitable for a particular vacancy you can reach out and discuss further with them. Facebook and Twitter are also options to think about. More and more businesses choose to advertise and recruit via social media, but when it comes to finding the best candidates, LinkedIn is definitely your go-to tool of choice.

Once you identify a candidate or client you want to discuss a potential working arrangement with, all of the above information we've talked about in this chapter applies. Building up a strong working relationship is based upon being human and speaking to them like people. If you start throwing around fancy language and speaking as though you're talking down to them, you're quickly going to lose their attention and they will seek out another recruitment company that is more people-orientated.

Remember to keep your efforts people-focused rather than number-focused. By doing that, the numbers will come on their own.

Chapter 4:

10 Office Tips to Boost Your Productivity

Recruitment can seem like you're juggling several balls in the air at one time. The problem is, if you drop one, you could risk losing a big client or a talented candidate.

The answer is to try and make more time during your working day, so that you're calm and in control of what you need to do.

Time management is vital for a recruiter. At any one time, you could be working on more than one project and that means you need to be organised and know exactly what needs to be done, without becoming confused or missing an important detail.

As your business grows, you may take on more employees to help you with the day to day running of your agency, but the chances are at the start that it will be you just you, or perhaps you and one other person. Trying to magically create more hours in the day is actually possible, but you need to make use of clever time saving tips in order to do it.

In this chapter, we will cover 10 tips you can use to boost your productivity in the office, and therefore create more hours in your working day. This will help you to feel more in control of your work, and as a result, you'll be more confident. This will show to your clients and candidates and ensure that you continue to attract more business to your company.

Tip 1 - Have Dual Monitors

It's a good idea both have a large desk with dual monitors. Trying to source candidates for a vacancy can be difficult when you're switching between your CMS and various other sites on your browser. Having dual screens means that you can have LinkedIn open permanently and you can have your CMS open on the other. You can then simply look at either screen when needed, rather than having to manually flick between the two.

This tip means that you can work faster and that you're also reducing the risk of making a mistake and entering the wrong information for the wrong person.

Tip 2 - Have a Cloud-Based CRM

Earlier in part one, we talked about the different types of CRM available. Whilst desktop CRMs and served-based options are viable, if you want to get more done in the time you have, a Cloud-based option is best. This also means that as you grow your business, and perhaps employ other people to help you run your business, you can all access the CRM without someone having to log off halfway through a task, so someone else can do what they need to do.

Productivity-wise, Cloud-based options are far more efficient.

Tip 3 - Have Flexible Working Hours

It's easy to work regular Monday to Friday, 9-5 hours but there are some clients who may be extremely busy during those hours and have no time to speak to you about their recruitment needs. Having flexible working hours, perhaps working 10 until 6 one day or maybe going into work an hour or two earlier means that you can catch the people you need to speak to during their quieter times, before the day really gets going, or as it is winding down. This could help you to catch new clients and therefore boost the success of your agency.

Tip 4 - Create a List of Priorities For The Day
Start every day by writing a list of the things you need to complete. It's very easy for a million and one things to crop up and take your attention away from the most important tasks, but by having a written reminder you won't forget. You could also set alerts on your phone or computer to remind you about these at specific times of the day.

Recruitment is extremely busy and there are times when two people will call you about totally different things and then your mind will completely forget the one thing you were working on. By having a priority list for each day, you'll ensure that your deadlines are met.

Tip 5 - Always Return Calls And Emails by The End of The Day

Never allow a call to be left until the next day or let an email go unanswered. It's a far better option to reply quickly to the email if you're busy and say that you have received their message and you will get back to them the next day. By doing that, you're acknowledging their concern and they will feel that you have everything under control. This also builds the level of trust we talked about in our last chapter.

It's also a good idea to make sure that any calls you received whilst you were out, missed or left messages on an answering machine, are all returned by the end of the day. People don't like to be left waiting and whilst their issue might not be that much of a priority to you, they don't see it that way. Even if you can't sort out their problem that particular day, returning their call and getting all the information you need will help them to have more faith in your abilities and therefore keep the quality of your working relationship high.

Tip 6 - Track How Much Time You Spend on Regular Tasks

As your recruitment company is starting to get off the ground, it's a good idea to identify tasks that you need to complete on a regular basis and then track how long they take you on average. You can then identify any areas that take too much time and look to streamline this, perhaps using a digitalised method or even outsourcing it to someone else if you just don't have the spare time to complete it to the desired standard.

Tip 7 - Declutter Your Browser Tabs With an Extension

Whilst you're sourcing candidates and working through the tasks you need to do, you'll probably find that you have a million and one tabs open on your browser. You can easily become confused and not be able to find what you're looking for and this can take a lot more time than if you were more streamlined in your approach.

A good way to counteract this is to install a free extension on your browser that declutters these open tabs and complies them into an easy to use list. You can then click on the page you want to see after you've finished what you're looking at, safe in the knowledge that you're not losing anything or forgetting anything.

The other plus point of using an extension such as this means that your computer will be faster because it clears up the memory space. A faster computer means the ability to do more in the time you have.

Tip 8 - Turn Off Your Email Notifications

The chances are that your email is going to be pinging all day long, but this is nothing but a distraction. Instead, schedule in time to check your emails perhaps three times a day - once in the morning, once after lunch, and once before you finish for the day. Obviously, make sure you reply to all before you log off for the evening. You can set alerts on your calendar to remind you, freeing up your attention to focus on the other tasks you need to do.

Tip 9 - Use a Chat Bot on Your Website

You might find that you're answering regular questions a lot and that these are eating into the amount of time you have during your working day. A good idea to save that time is to install a chat bot on your website. This will answer frequently asked questions and is there to help your visitors 24 hours a day. As a result, your customers get the answers they need, they don't have to wait for them, and you're not having your time cut short by answering regular and simple questions.

Tip 10 - Schedule Your Days Carefully

One of the biggest scheduling mistakes you can commit is to forget travelling time when visiting clients and overstretch yourself during your working day. If you do have to travel to visit someone, make sure that you factor in enough time to travel there and back, schedule a lunch break to refresh your mind, and also make sure that every day has a section of time blocked out for admin tasks. By staying on top of your general admin, you'll find that your business runs far smoother and you'll save time in the long-run too.

These 10 productivity tips can easily be used from the start of your recruitment company's first day. Keeping them in mind means that you'll save time, you'll have more space to get on with the things you need to do, you won't forget anything important and your clients and candidates won't feel forgotten.

Chapter 5:

10 Recruitment-Specific Good Practice Tips to Use at All Times

Running a successful recruitment company covers a huge range of different facets, and in our last chapter, we talked about how to make more time throughout the day with a few time management tips. In this chapter, we're going to take it a step further and talk about good practice tips that are recruitment-specific.

Good practice means that you're not only being efficient, but you're being professional too. It shows your clients and candidates that you are high quality and that you know exactly what you're doing. That reassurance puts them at ease and helps them to refer your services to other people they're connected with.

With that in mind, let's look at 10 recruitment-specific tips that ensure good practice.

Tip 1 - Always Set Follow up Reminders

Reach out to a client or a candidate is one thing but you need to remember to follow up your conversation a few days later. This isn't an aggressive approach, it's simply mopping up and ensuring that you gain the answers you need in order to move forwards with the work you need to do. Perhaps a client said that they needed to discuss their next move with a manager or Board member and they would get back to you, but they haven't. That's your cue to call them and enquire about progress.

It's easy to forget to do this because you're so busy, but that's where you should be setting reminders on your calendar. Don't be too quick to follow up, give it a few days and then simply drop them a line and ask to speak to the same person you discussed things with last time. The same goes for candidates who appear on the fence about whether to apply for a job or not - schedule ten minutes or so in a few days' time to call them back and follow up.

Tip 2 - Check Everyone is Still Attending on The Morning of an Interview

It doesn't look good if a candidate you were hoping would shine at interview simply doesn't turn up, either because they forgot or because they changed their mind. Make sure you give all your interviewees a quick reminder call or message on the morning of the interview and check they reply.

Someone can forget an interview for many different reasons, or it could be that they're having a last minute bout of nerves. In that case, you can talk them around and make sure that they attend. Remember, people skills are vital and sometimes that means boosting someone's confidence when it might be lacking a little - if you have faith in your candidates, they will too.

Tip 3 - Always Give Feedback

Whether or not a candidate is successful, always give feedback. Your candidate may be able to learn from that feedback, which will help them get the job they want the next time. Also, don't keep your candidates waiting too long to let them know whether or not they were successful. It's not difficult to give everyone on your list a quick phone call after the decision has been made, and it's better than writing "I'm sorry to let you know ..." letter which takes days to arrive. Put yourself in the shoes of the candidate and appreciate that they want to know sooner rather than later and if they're not successful, they may want to know why.

Tip 4 - Consider Score Cards at Interviews

Whilst you'll have standard questions to ask at interview, much of it goes on a gut feeling too. However, gut feelings aren't always accurate and that means you should have score cards. This rates candidates on their responses to important questions, and helps you to pull out the highlights of their interview against any potential downsides.

Tip 5 - Stay in Touch With Candidates

Just because a candidate wasn't ideal for one particular job, it doesn't mean they won't be completely perfect for another. Stay in touch with your candidates and inform them of any roles coming up that may suit them better.

Tip 6 - Make Sure Candidates Have a Good Experience With You

It's worth remembering that candidates can sign up with as many recruitment agencies as they like, so you're always in competition against others when it comes to the preferences of your candidates. For this reason, you should make sure your candidate has a good experience with you and that you focus on their job-seeking needs.

It's true that clients and candidates are equally as important as one another, but without candidates, who are you going to get to fill the vacancies your clients need to be filled? Make sure their experience is a good one and they'll be more excited about the vacancies you pitch to them.

Tip 7 - Be Regularly Active on Social Media

Social media marketing will turn out to be one of the main channels for approaching and attracting clients and candidates so make sure that you're active on a regular basis. It's a good idea to schedule in an hour or so every day to check social media channels and perhaps post updates, etc. This keeps everyone in the loop about your business and ensure that you're at the forefront of their mind, compared to everyone else.

Tip 8 - Don't Simply Cast Aside CVs With Gaps

Sometimes a fantastic candidate will come along and everything is perfect, until you see their CV and you notice several gaps in it. You might be tempted to cast it aside for this reason, but instead of doing that, make sure you give them a call and try and find out the reason for the gaps.

There might be a very acceptable reason, such as illness, caring for a relative, travel, etc. Rather than just casting it to one side, ask the appropriate questions and help them to make their CV look

more presentable with the information they give to
you.

Tip 9 - Always Ask For ID

Don't make the rookie mistake of simply assuming
that someone is able to work in the UK or that
they are who they say they are. Of course, most of
the time everyone is going to be upfront and honest
but you have a duty to ensure that you are working
with candidates who have the right to work n the
UK and has the right paperwork to back this up.

The best practice here is to ask everyone to provide
identification and papers to prove their right to
work in the UK. For British nationals, this will
obviously be their passport as proof of birth in the
UK, but for anyone else, you will need to see back-
up papers and you'll also need to keep a copy on
file.

**Tip 10 - Make Sure You Tailor Your Interview
Questions Beforehand**

It's a huge mistake to have a bank of interview
questions that you just use every single time for any
interview. Every job is subtly different and you will
need to ask pertinent questions to ensure you find
the right candidate for the job. This means you
need to create a list of interview questions before

the day and tweak them in the days leading up to the interview, if any new ideas come to your mind.

Taking these 10 best practice tips into account will help you to streamline your working practices and will also help to boost your profile with clients and candidates. The more professional you are and appear, the more you're going to attract business to your recruitment agency, and make it more likely that you're going to be chosen over the competition.

Summing up Part 2

This part has been about running a successful recruitment company. In the early months of starting your business, you will make the odd mistake, you'll learn from it, and you'll find new ways to approach different tasks.

Recruitment can be very busy and it can mean that you're juggling several different tasks in the air. Whilst multitasking might seem like the obvious answer to this, remember that multitasking in itself can be a problem; sometimes it's far better to complete one task before moving onto the next, rather than trying to juggle ten balls and potentially drop a few along the way.

Managing your time and focusing on best practice procedures means that you'll have more time to focus on your clients and customers, therefore working on developing those strong working relationships. A recruiter who is always behind, always trying to catch up, and constantly stressed out and busy is not going to be able to provide the best service. This will also show to clients and candidates, who perhaps just want five minutes of your time to discuss a small issue they have.

Remember, recruitment is an extremely competitive industry and in order to shine, you need to appear completely in control. The tips we've covered in this second part of the book will enable you to do that, and feel more confident in your abilities as a result.

In our third and final part, we are going to discuss future business growth, and how you can take your current, relatively small agency and build it into a business empire to be reckoned with!

PART 3
GROWING YOUR BUSINESS

Chapter 1:

The Importance of Staying Relevant

The recruitment industry is extremely competitive and it seems like almost every month a new agency appears on the block. Candidates can choose to work with several agencies if they choose to and they're more likely to be picky when it comes to those who can provide them with what they need.

In addition, technology is constantly evolving and changing, which means they need to stay ahead of the game and always look to develop your current practices. Choosing one CMS that works for you is a good option at the start, but you should always be open to adding new technological advancements into your business practices. Failure to do this means that other businesses may be more effective and may be able to demand the attention of top quality talent.

At the end of the day, the company with the best talent on the books is the one that wins.

Of course, business growth is vital for any business, no matter what type of industry they're in. If you remain static, you will eventually start to see a downturn on your fortunes, and that is extremely pertinent when it comes to the extremely competitive nature of the recruitment business.

Growth is vital for the long-term survival of any business. There are many benefits of focusing on this, not least the fact that a growing business, which shows a constant evolution and upturn in profits finds it easier to secure new funding, assets, attracts new talent to work for the company and also secures a far more impressive reputation. As we've mentioned several times already, reputation is everything in the recruitment industry.

Put simply, business growth pushes forth performance, productivity and therefore profits.

There are several ways you can focus on growing your recruitment agency, such as moving into new specialisms, but the most effective methods are often the simplest. This includes focusing on your clients and ensuring that your social media presence is strong enough. In this final part of the book, we will talk about the best ways to grow your business towards future success.

International Hiring

Many recruitment agencies hire international candidates for roles. If you're not yet doing this, you may be missing out on something which can help you to increase your business share and access impressive talent for the vacancies you're trying to fill.

Of course, international hiring does come with a few issues that you need to be extremely aware of. The code of practice we talked about in our first part mentioned that any recruitment must be ethical. You need to see proof of someone's ability to work in the UK, and you should keep a copy of these documents on file. It's good practice to ask everyone for this information, but when hiring internationally, this is even more important.

Finding international clients rests solely on social media marketing. Social media allows you to reach out to far more people than you would otherwise be able to contact, so ensuring that you focus on your social media platforms is vital. Casting your net a little wider is a good way to increase the quality of your agency via the candidates it provides to clients.

Obviously, this may provide a few challenges in terms of interviews, however. This is a hurdle you can overcome by offering video interviews over Zoom or Skype, which will allow international candidates to have an equal chance of being successful as those who are able to attend in person.

Change Your Niche

At the start of your business, when you were setting everything up, you might have chosen one particular specialism. Whilst you would have chosen that specialist for a specific reason, e.g. you have in-depth knowledge of that particular niche, it's a good idea to look at expanding your niche choice a little further.

You don't have to be completely generalised, but if you are too rigid in the types of clients you're looking to work with, you may find that you're cutting off several other options that may be quite profitable and could bring you increased workload in the future.

Whilst being experienced in a specific niche will allow you to demand higher fees, the demand for that particular role may not be as great as you perhaps thought at the start. In addition, it could be that you're simply not making enough profits or gaining enough clients by being this rigid in your business choices.

Opening up your choice of niche means that you have a greater choice of clients and you also increase your experience level. You can link the niche to the one you are currently working with, or you can open it up even more.

It's a personal choice, but being too rigid with your niche choice could mean that you are missing out on business and therefore not allowing your reputation to spread as far as it may otherwise do.

Keep Your Focus on Why You're Doing it

Feedback from many successful recruitment businesses all points to one very important piece of advice - always remember why you're doing it.

If you're passionate about what you're doing, it's never going to become old. You can easily try new things and push the boundaries, but if you forget your reason for starting in the first place, you're going to lose your way.

This is where a mission statement comes in very useful.

Quality businesses all have mission statements. This means that you are able to refer to your reason for being and you will keep it in mind at all times. It ensures that your employees are all working towards a common goal and your customers know what you are about. This helps to give you an identity and ensure that you never stray far from your core reason for being.

Having a 'why' is also very important when things are difficult.

We've already mentioned that recruitment is competitive and that means there will always be times when things don't go according to plan, you might lose a client to a competitor, or a top candidate you were banking on chooses not to sign up with your agency. These are hurdles that befall every single recruitment business, but your why will keep you on track and allow you to be motivated towards future improvement.

It's vital to ensure that every single mistake or problem you encounter is reviewed and learned from. Have regular assessments and identify problems that may have come your way during a set amount of time. This will give you the chance to look at particular issues, break them down, figure out why they happened, and then learn how to overcome them for the next time, or stop them happening again completely.

As your business grows, you could also set up focus groups from your employees to help work on these problems and understand what you can do better next time.

A high quality recruitment company knows that you can never stop learning, improving and striving to be better. So, rather than seeing problems as serious issues and annoyances, welcome them as learning opportunities instead.

The Client is Always Right

You may not agree that the client is right, but if you want to grow your business, you have to adopt this mindset.

If you want your business to succeed you have to do everything you can to help the client feel that they're valued, listened to, and that you're providing them with the very best service you can. This service has to be better than an experience they've had with a previous client and it has to be better than anything they think they could get from one of your competitors.

Building high quality relationships with your clients is one of the best ways to grow your business. From there, they will tell their business friends about your services, and you'll receive word of mouth referrals, which can often turn into new business in the near future.

Achieving this aim isn't difficult, and it really comes down to regular communication, listening to the needs of your client, visiting them in person whenever you can, keeping them updated on anything they need to know, and ensuring that you do your very best for them, every single time. Going above and beyond is the sign of a high quality recruitment business and one which will always out-perform its competitors.

This chapter has talked about a few of the basics that help your business to grow. From this point, we'll delve a little deeper and give you some practice advice to focus on.

Chapter 2:

8 Tips to Expand Your Recruitment Agency

We've generalised up to now, but we now need to delve a little deeper and talk about the finer details you can use to try and build your business and grow your brand.

Again, these tips aren't extremely difficult to do, as you're already doing a lot of the positive things already if you've followed the advice we've given already in the book. When growing your business you need to take things a step further, hustle and focus on improvement wherever possible.

Let's look at 8 tips you can use to expand your recruitment agency.

Tip 1 - Hire The Right People

As your business grows, so will your workload and that means you'll be juggling a million balls in the air. It's not possible to provide the best service if you're not focused and if you don't have the time to concentrate on one thing at a time. In that case, consider hiring employees to help you with your workload. However, make sure that you hire the right people for the job.

Recruitment is your specialism, so this shouldn't be too hard for you! You need people you can trust, who you get along well with, and those who have an equal passion for the role as you do. Once you identify the right people for the role, trust them to do their job and don't look over their shoulder all the time or try to micromanage - that's not the point of hiring someone and it's very counterproductive!

Hire the right amount of people you need, and don't be too worried about numbers. If you can justify the employees you take on, and if the quality of the service you provide to clients increases as a result, it's a good decision. However, it's also a good idea to ensure that one person deals with one client. Clients like consistency and that means whenever they have an issue they know they can speak to the one person who is covering their case and who knows it inside out. If you're constantly switching between employees and having to catch everyone up and how things are progressing with that vacancy, you're wasting time, you're risking work being done twice, and you're increasing the risk of misunderstandings or mistakes occurring.

Take your time finding the right people to help you run your recruitment business and the future results will be more than worth the effort.

Tip 2 - Update Your Infrastructure on a Regular Basis

Your infrastructure is how you do your work, the CMS you use, the methods you use to find candidates and how you make your entire system work. Whilst it's probably doing very well for you right now, that doesn't mean it's always going to be that way, and you should always be on the look out for ways it can improve or be updated.

The recruitment agency is fast moving and never stands still for very long. It's also fierce in terms of competition and if you want to remain in front of your competitors and not quickly lagging behind, you need to focus on keeping your infrastructure, fresh, strong, and effective.

If you've found a CMS that really works well for you, you don't have to change it, but you should look towards other methods that might improve the way you work. This could include having dual monitors, as we mentioned in one of our tips earlier, or it could be completely overhauling the way you work after having a sneak peek at a new computer system which you know could bring great results.

Don't be afraid to make changes to your infrastructure if needs be. The old 'if it ain't broke, don't fix it' adage doesn't really apply to the recruitment industry - you cannot stand still for too long.

Tip 3 - Outsource The Things You Don't Have Time For

Streamlining your working practices makes you more effective and efficient, therefore helping your business to grow far faster as a result. One way to do that is to look at your business practices and outsource anything that you simply don't have the time for, or anything which you don't have the greatest amount of knowledge of.

In our first part, we talked about outsourcing your website design needs, but we also talked about outsourcing your content writing to a writer who understands SEO. This is the perfect example; a freelance writer has specialist skills and can take your SEO marketing to a greater level. If you try to do it, you may miss several important points, simply because it's not something that you have in-depth knowledge of at this point. Sure, you can teach yourself, but it takes time.

By outsourcing, you'll gain greater results in less time and that allows your business to develop and grow much faster than it would do otherwise. Yes, you will need to pay your freelancers, but that is a minimal amount when you consider the cash you will lose in terms of time if you attempt to do everything yourself.

You can outsource anything you want, but make sure that you keep the basic reins of the business firmly in your hands. You don't want to lose the personalised approach for your clients. Accounting is definitely something you should outsource to your accountant, but you can also outsource employee payroll too, if you find that you just don't have the time or expertise to do it. Content writing, website updates, social media marketing and graphic design for any marketing campaigns are also things you can outsource.

Tip 4 - Improve Your Digital Marketing Approach

The recruitment world is increasingly online. That means that your marketing needs to be aimed towards the online world too.

If you took notice of our advice on how to set up and run your recruitment agency in a successful manner, you'll know that you need a digital marketing strategy in place. That also means that you need to update it regularly and make changes to things that may not be working as well as they could be.

Social media marketing methods can be reviewed regularly due to metrics, and these can show you how many leads you're receiving, how many turn into actual customers, and which platforms are working better than others.

If you don't have a blog already, it's time to set one up. This allows you to connect with your clients and candidates in a way that you wouldn't have been able to do before. If you already have a blog, how about outsourcing it to a freelancer, to free up your time and ensure that it is maximised in terms of quality. You should also add some video content to your social media marketing, to make your platforms more immersive and innovative.

Constantly evaluating your digital marketing plan means that you can get the most out of it, and when you do that, the potential for success is extremely large.

Tip 5 - Establish a Firm Brand Identity

Having a brand identity means that you're noticed, people know who you are, and your names comes up when the subject of recruitment is discussed. These are all important ticks to have at the side of your name and will ensure that you receive more clients and candidates as a result.

People like to work with established, credible businesses. This gives them a sense of reassurance that they know what they're getting and that the final outcome is going to be exactly what they need. They also want to know that working with you is going to be easy, that you make the whole process much simpler than if they were trying to navigate their way through it themselves.

Building your brand covers a wide range of tasks, but being true to your business is vital. This means being consistent. Make sure that your website reflects who you are as a business and the design is in-keeping with what you're doing. That goes for all your social media posts and blog as well. If you have business cards, make sure they are consistent in design. In addition, consider doing some charitable work to build up your name and your brand, perhaps sponsoring a local community charity or regularly donating to a larger charity.

Establishing your brand identity means being true to it at all times and not deviating off on a tangent into unknown territory. If you write in the first person your website, as though you are chatting to your customers, make sure that is consistent throughout all your communication efforts. If you write in the third person, make sure you're consistent with that.

Have a logo that is innovative and tells people who you are and show it on all your correspondence and your website. Get the word out and make sure that you do exactly as you say you're going to do. This helps you to build your business because people get to know you and they know what to expect from you.

Tip 6 - Never Assume You Know it All

One of the most important things to remember with recruitment is that you can never know it all. This is a fast-moving business, one which will quickly leave you behind if you assume that you don't need to keep evolving and changing to meet industry demands. Don't be so closed-minded that you think you've done all the research you need to do and that's it, you're set for the rest of your business' lifespan.

A high quality recruiter is always open to change and always keen to learn more. Read up on industry news, attend conferences and learn about new technology that may help in your day to day work. Listen to your employees and ask for their opinions on how things could be improved around the office. Being open to new ideas and new approaches shows that you're keen to grow and it will give you the very best shot at improving upon your current situation.

Even the most experienced recruiters know that there is always room for new knowledge and that changing things isn't something to be feared. Take a leaf out of their book.

Tip 7 - Get Out And Meet People

The fact that the recruitment industry is so online-based these days makes it easy to simply sit in your office and answer messages, emails and phone calls, but it's a good idea to make sure you're visible too. Get out of the office and go and see your clients, meet them in person and let them get to see your personality and your determination to find them the best candidates. Similarly, meet up with candidates and invite them into the office, or have open days.

Being more present and approachable builds up that all-important bond of trust and in the recruitment business, as we've already explored, that is a vital point to tick off the list.

Before clients even sign up with your company, make a point of going to see them in person. Make an appointment and sell your services. This could be the difference between them passing on your services this time, or taking them up. When someone makes an effort to be visible and to show you what they can do, you're far more likely to be convinced that they're the ones you should be working with.

Tip 8 - Attend Conferences/Events And Network

Make sure that you are on LinkedIn as well as the other main social media platforms, so that potential clients and candidates can find you themselves, but you should also be out there networking on a regular basis. There are many recruitment events going on throughout the year, so make sure you note these down on your calendar and attend as many as you can in person.

Whilst you're at these events, have a supply of business cards ready to go and hand them out to those you meet. Don't be afraid to speak to people you don't know or those who may seem more experienced than you. Even if you don't receive any business from your networking on one occasion, you may still meet someone with a lot more experience who could almost provide a mentor-style role.

In any people-oriented business, networking is vital.

These 8 tips on how to grow your business aren't particularly technical, but they work extremely well. When working in recruitment, you're working with people and providing a service. That means you need to focus on how you treat people, allow word of mouth to spread, and do your best to help boost it along the way.

In our next chapter we're going to talk about how you monitor your growth, and know where to make any necessary changes.

Chapter 3:

How Key Performance Indicators (KPIs) Can Help You

Earlier in our book, we talked about areas to monitor to ensure that your business is running successfully. There are also areas you need to monitor and check regularly to ensure that your business is growing. These are known as Key Performance Indicators, or KPIs for short.

There are countless KPIs you can look at and try and decipher, but it's best to stick to the ones which yield the most pertinent information where growth is concerned. By keeping an eye on these KPIs and looking for upward or downward trends, you can work out whether any improvements need to be made. You can also estimate how much growth you can look forward to within that quarter of the year.

KPIs shouldn't be your sole point to consider when thinking about growth. It's sometimes very easy to notice whether or not your business is growing because you can see it in your profits, but there are also subtle signs that you may miss, simply because you're so focused on keeping your business going and working hard.

KPIs can give you important information but don't become too obsessed with their meaning. Use them to look for trends and use them to inform you of areas that need to be improved.

Every business has a set of KPIs they use to measure how things are going, but in the recruitment business, there is a huge list of areas you can use in this regard. For that reason, stick to the easiest to decipher, to save you time and energy.

KPIs to Monitor Regularly

The following KPIs should be on your radar and checked on a regular basis.

Time to Hire

The time to hire KPI is measured by looking at the date a candidate was hired and taking the number of days or months away from the date their details were entered into your CMS database. This basically tells you how long it has taken to get them a job they were suitable for.

This particular KPI helps you to make changes to your hiring process by looking for common problems. On average, time to fill a position can take between 2 weeks to 63 days, but the slower the time, the more damaging it can be for your reputation. Also, whilst you're taking your time screening and interviewing candidates, one of your competitors could be working at a faster pace and offering an attractive role to a candidate you also have signed up. In that case, of course, they're going to be more likely to take the job they're offered, rather than wait to see what happens with your process.

Quality of Hire

To measure the quality of hire KPI you need to also breakdown and measure the individual performance, productivity and retention rate of a particular candidate. The overall score gives you the quality of hire. It's obviously far better to have high scores here because it shows that your recruitment skills are top-notch and you are able to identify the best candidates for vacancies. It also helps to ensure that clients can see your skills ensures high retention rates, which saves time and money in the long-run. Remember, candidates who are successful but then leave the job quickly can damage your reputation because you sourced them out in the first place!

A regular turnover of candidates shows that perhaps your screening and interviewing processes aren't as high quality as they could and should be.

Sourcing Channel Efficiency

This KPI helps you to identify where you're getting your best candidates from and any areas which need to be improved, e.g. particular social media platforms.

To calculate this KPI you will need to have an average number of conversions from a specific platform, e.g. Facebook and then subtract it from the average number of conversations from all platforms. This will then tell you how successful Facebook is against the rest of your social media or other platforms. You can then repeat the process with the others, to work out which one is the most successful versus the least. You can also easily work out where the majority of your candidates are coming from by using this KPI, be it job board, referrals, social media, or LinkedIn, etc.

This particular KPI is useful for helping you to work out whether you need to put more work into a specific platform or area, in order to increase the number of conversations, i.e. the number of candidates you sourced from that particular platform or area.

You can easily continue on for hours with more potential KPIs to monitor, but your working days are busy enough without adding more work to your list. These KPIs are enough to tell you whether growth is occurring and at what rate, as well as any areas you need to work on. Of course, perhaps the easiest KPI of all to look at is profits and compare this quarter's profits against last quarter's.

Quarterly Reviews

It's important to check your KPIs on a regular basis, but not too regularly. If you don't leave enough time between your reviews, you're not going to see the whole picture and you won't know what you need to work on versus what is working well for you. For that reason, quarterly reviews are a good idea.

This means that every four months you will block out some time in your schedule, work out your KPIs and compare them against those from the last quarter. Over the space two or more quarters, you'll be able to identify the rate of growth that you're experiencing. If it's good news for you, you simply need to keep doing what you're doing and looking for more ways to improve, but if you're noticing a downward trend or the rate isn't as fast as you would like, you need to sit down and work out what needs to be worked on and what may not be currently working for you.

Chapter 4:

Four Simple Steps to Business Growth

There are four specific steps that create almost guaranteed business growth. These steps encompass many of the points we've talked about so far in this chapter but give you an overview of what you need to do to create a satisfactory rate of growth.

The four main steps are:

1. Obtain more of the types of clients that you want and need
2. Ensure that clients come back to you multiple times
3. Create an increased value on every successful hire you make
4. Make sure that your processes are constantly improved in terms of effectiveness

In this final chapter, we will talk more about how to achieve these steps and therefore, in line with the other tips we've given you, you should notice that your recruitment business increases year upon year.

Identify The Clients You Want

When sourcing out clients to work with, any client is not as good as the right type of client. If you want to focus on business growth, you need to make sure that you focus on quality, not quantity. Sure, more clients might seem like a good idea, because that means you can charge more fees, but lower fees and more hassle might not turn out to be the most productive use of your time.

Try to identify the types of clients that you really want to work with. Perhaps you've worked with some high quality clients in the past and you'd like to repeat that type of experience, or maybe you've had a bad experience and you know what you want to avoid.

This also means that you need to understand your niche very well and do some more market research. By doing this you can understand the needs of your ideal type of client and as a result, you can tailor your recruitment approach towards them. Then, become an expert in those areas by showcasing your skills with a strong online presence and being visible at trade events. As we mentioned before, networking is vital, especially if you want to work with the right types of clients for you.

Once you've identified a potential client approach them and use your USP to get their attention. Sell your skills and make sure they're very aware of what you can give to them. Don't give up, make sure that you follow up any conversations a few days later and continue to highlight the plus points of working with you.

Once you have signed up a client that is your ideal model type, keep a track on what you did and what works well versus what didn't. Then, you know how to replicate your success with other clients.

Focus on Repeat Business

Once you have worked with your ideal type of client, you'll certainly want them to come back to you time and time again. This means you've built up a bond of trust and a strong working relationship. It also means that they're also more likely to refer your services to their friends and colleagues who may be in need of recruitment help.

However, just because a client was thrilled with the experience, it doesn't mean they're 100% going to come back to you the next time they have a recruitment vacancy to fill. They may decide to fill it internally, they might choose to do the recruitment themselves to save money, or they may have their head turned by one of your competitors.

That means you need to focus on ensuring that high quality clients return to you when they need your services once more. You can do that with the following points:

- Make sure that you focus on giving the best quality service possible to every single client
- Keep the contract beneficial and add value, without contacting them every single second of the day. Update them regularly via newsletters and emails, social media, etc, but not to the point of annoyance
- Ask for feedback from clients which can be added to your website
- Check in with your client at a later date, to remind them of your existence and to prompt them to contact you at any point when they need a vacancy filling.

Increase The Value of Each Placement

Every single sale, or placement, you create you need to try and increase the value of it time after time. Of course, you will have a set fee that is charged to them, but there are ways to try and get more form each placement, without actually increasing the fee you charge to your clients.

If you constantly 'up' your fees, clients are probably going to go elsewhere, because everyone wants to have high quality at the lowest possible price. With that in mind, check out the following ways to get more value from a contract.

- By impressing clients with your skills and outcomes from previous placements, you can aim to become the person they go to when they need vacancies of a higher salary amount filling. This means you increase the amount of profit, simply because your fee will be higher
- Think about adding in extras to your services, such as skills testing or personality assessments. The more extras you can provide, you can add in extra fees to cover the cost. This will however mean that you have to work with another company that provides these tests, and they will require their share of the extra fee.

Improve Your Effectiveness Time Over Time

Every single step in your recruitment process needs to be as effective as possible, so it costs less to perform. That means you're saving money and it will contribute to the overall growth of your business. This also frees up extra time so you can focus on other things, such as sourcing other ideal clients to add to your books.

Your processes need to be as strong as they possibly can be and this means having the right technology and mechanisms in place to cover each step carefully. Its good practice to have a template for each step in your process and a series of tick boxes that need to be achieved. This will create the best outcome every single time.

Remember, you don't know everything, so make sure that you outsource where necessary and that you liaise with your employees and delegate tasks which they are particularly skilled at. It could be that one of your employees is fantastic with social media marketing or another aspect of the recruitment process, so maximise their skills and free up your own time along the way.

It's also important that you remain up to date with new industry news, updates and technology, and to utilise these updates as much as possible. Encourage your employees to read up on the latest industry news and to bring to the table anything they feel could be useful for your business as a whole.

The more effective ever single step of your recruitment process, the happier your clients, the ore they will return to you, and they will also refer your services to their colleagues.

These four steps add up to the perfect storm where business growth is concerned. With more clients on your books who are looking to recruit to higher salaried vacancies, the higher the fees you can charge, more profits come your way, an increased reputation, most importantly, business growth.

Summing up Part 3

Growth is vital for every business. Without growth, you're quickly going to become static and your competitors will overtake you, taking clients with them and leaving you with very little left to choose from.

As a recruitment business, you need to be one step ahead of the game at all times. This is an industry that moves fast, and if you don't make a very concerted effort to remain up to date, you're going to notice decline, rather than growth.

In this chapter, we've talked about the main ways to ensure that your business grows year upon year, and much of that is down to how you treat your clients and your candidates. In a person-facing business such as this, you need to remember that basic manners, courtesy, respect, and value go a long, long way. One simple misunderstanding, due to unclear communication, can cause a client to feel that they no longer want to work with you, causing them to approach one of your competitors the next time they have a vacancy they want to fill.

Of course, it's about more than that too. It's also about how you improve your processes and commit to staying up to date and innovative. When you combine these two efforts, whilst also ensuring that you regularly review Key Performance Indicators (KPIs), you will be able to identify what needs to change versus what is working very well for you as it is.

Successful recruitment company owners know that they can never rest on their laurels for very long. In this industry, you need to keep moving, keep hustling, and always remain one step ahead if you want to be a success.

Conclusion

Recruitment is an industry that will challenge even the most experienced business owner. It is one of the fastest growing industries in the country, and with more and more businesses of this nature popping up, that means you need to identify your Unique Selling Point (USP) and use it time and time again to create an irresistible force in your direction.

Throughout this book, we have given you all the information you need to set up your recruitment business from scratch, create a successful picture from the start, and then we've talked about how to continue the story and grow your business into the years to come.

However, do not assume that your story is going to be easy and that there will never be any issues, hurdles, or roadblocks along the way. The key to overcoming these is to have faith in your journey, to know what you're working for, and to ensure that your brand identity is strong enough to survive any storm.

You might think that the hardest part of the journey is setting up your business, but that's actually the easiest part, because there are clear steps to take which will get you where you need to be, with little to get in the way. The hard work starts when you try to secure your first client and whilst you're working on your first project. Then, you need to constantly move to try and update and improve your processes, to ensure that clients come back to you, that you can secure projects with higher fees, and all the while creating the ideal working relationship with your clients and candidates.

Whilst this is going on, you also need to have a very strong digital marketing plan in place, which ensures that you have a strong online presence that can't be broken. Recruitment is increasingly an online-style of business and whilst you should never underestimate the power of face to face and voice contact, finding clients and candidates is often done online. Without a strong presence in the online world, you're missing out in a big way.

Despite the fact that recruitment is hard work, it is also very rewarding. This is a business that allows you to help candidates reach their potential and find a role that they're truly happy with. It also allows you to improve businesses by finding the ideal person for their vacant jobs. As a result, you have the power to create real change, but you have to dedicate the right amount of time, effort, and skills to do the very best you can do.

Your Journey Starts Here

The best advice is to take your time when setting up your business. Focus on covering all the initial steps to ensure that you don't miss anything important. It's especially vital that you register your business correctly and register for tax and VAT with HMRC. Failure to do this quickly could land you in trouble before you even get started.

Remember that the foundations will influence the rest of your business and whether or not it grows in a steady rate or not. Choose a name that is easily able to translate into the future, and focus on understanding the market as best you can before you make a move. Do as much market research as you can, learn and ask for advice, and never assume that you know more than you do. If you can find a mentor within the recruitment industry to help you out in the early stages, that could certainly serve you well.

It's worthwhile investing in the design of your website and spending a little more on a high quality CMS to get you started. This means you can hit the ground running and you won't run into as many initial hiccups as you may otherwise do.

When your business is registered and set up, you're ready to start sourcing clients and then, top talent candidates to fill the jobs you have. Your online presence will help you with this, so again, focus heavily on that and if you need to outsource to give you a strong platform on which to build, do so.

Always remember that recruitment is a person-facing business. You're providing a service for people and that means you need to communicate effectively, treat people how you would want to be treated, respect them, involve them, keep them updated, and listen to their wants, needs, and views. The best recruitment companies understand that the basics of how you treat a client and a candidate have a huge bearing on whether or not your business is a success first and foremost, and whether you experience business growth too.

All that is left to do is wish you luck with your new business venture. You're entering into an extremely competitive industry, but one which will bring you a huge sense of achievement with every successful hire made with your help.

A Short message from the Author:

Hey, are you enjoying the book? I'd love to hear your thoughts!

Many readers do not know how hard reviews are to come by, and how much they help an author.

I would be incredibly thankful if you could take just 60 seconds to write a brief review on Amazon, even if it's just a few sentences!

You can leave a review under the Orders page, at the links below.

https://www.amazon.com/your-account
https://www.amazon.co.uk/your-account

Thank you for taking the time to share your thoughts!